# Australian Labradoodles

a Labrador Retriever, Curly Coated Retriever, Irish Water Spaniel, American Cocker Spaniel, English Cocker Spaniel and Poodle Hybrid

The Ultimate
AUSTRALIAN LABRADOODLE
Dog Manual

Australian Labradoodle book for care, costs, feeding, grooming, health and training.

by

George Hoppendale

and

Asia Moore

**The Ultimate Australian Labradoodle Dog Manual**

Author: George Hoppendale
Author: Asia Moore – "*Ask a Dog Whisperer*"
www.k-9superheroesdogwhispering.com
Manager, Dogalize North America www.dogalize.com

Published by: Zoodoo Publishing

# Table of Contents

# About the Authors

George Hoppendale is an experienced writer and a true animal lover. He enjoys writing animal books and advising others how to take care of their animals to give them a happy home.

Asia Moore is an animal lover, professional Dog Whisperer, Cynologist, experienced Author and Manager for Dogalize North America, the free social media App for dog lovers, that puts all the things you want and everything you need for you and your dog conveniently together in one place.

Asia lives on Vancouver Island, off the west coast of British Columbia, in Canada, and believes that with the right training, all humans and dogs can live together in harmony.

She and her dog whispering detective team, which includes an 8-year-old Shih Tzu named Boris, train humans and rehabilitate canines by teaching dog psychology to human guardians, in order to prevent or help alleviate problem behaviors that arise through common as well as unusual misunderstandings between humans and their canine counterparts so that everyone can live a happy and stress-free life together.

Visit Asia and her dog whispering team online at:
**www.K-9SuperHeroesDogWhispering.com**

# Chapter 1: Introduction

It's important to gather as much information as possible before you take the plunge to share your home with a furry friend.

The Ultimate Australian Labradoodle Dog Manual will answer the questions you may have when researching this hybrid canine. If you are considering sharing your home with the active and intelligent, water loving Labrador Retriever, Curly Coated Retriever, Irish Water Spaniel, American & English Cocker Spaniel and Poodle mixed breed, this Manual is for you.

Learn all about this designer canine, including facts and secrets about all breeds that make up the Australian Labradoodle, and how to care for every stage of the Australian Labradoodle's life.

This Manual contains all the information you need, from choosing a breeder and finding the perfect puppy to how to care for an aging dog.

As well, you will learn about transitioning through house breaking, adolescence, daily care, health problem inherent in each parent breed, feeding, grooming, training, first commands and hand signals and end of life, so that you can make an educated decision when deciding whether or not the intelligent and energetic Australian Labradoodle designer dog is the breed for you and your family.

As well, this manual contains valuable information, tips and tricks that can easily be applied to any breed of canine.

# Chapter 2: The Australian Labradoodle

Currently the *"Australian Labradoodle"* is a cross between a Labrador Retriever, a Curly Coated Retriever, an Irish Water Spaniel, an American Cocker Spaniel, an English Cocker Spaniel and a Poodle.

The Australian Labradoodle is a hybrid, or designer dog bred in Australia and recognized by both the Labradoodle Association of Australia and the International Australian Labradoodle Association, Inc.

The first Australian Labradoodle breed standard was written in 1997 and since 2004 the Australian Labradoodle has been recognized by developers as a breed in its own right that has been carefully developed over many years with a view to achieving specific, agreed upon goals.

Depending upon whether the Australian Labradoodle is of Standard or Miniature size, this dog is usually going to weigh between 30 and 77 pounds (14 and 35 kilograms) and will stand between 17 and 24 inches (44 and 60 centimeters).

When two or more purebred canines are bred together, in the past they were simply referred to as *"mutts"*. Now, when two separate breeds are intentionally crossed or mixed together, they are often referred to as *"designer"* or *"hybrid"* dogs.

However, now that the Australian breeders have created a standard for the Australian Labradoodle, they may soon be ranked as a breed unto itself, and registered with the major kennel clubs as such.

In most cases, the obvious mark of a *"designer"* or *"hybrid"* dog' is that the resulting puppies are named with what is referred to as a *"portmanteau"* word, which is a word that is a combination of two or more words, syllables or sounds that have been taken from the names of the two or more purebred parents, that becomes the new name of the designer breed.

The term "hybrid" or *"designer dog"* began during the late 20th century, when breeders first began to intentionally mix "Poodles" with other types of purebred canines with the intent of creating offspring that would retain the hypoallergenic "Poodle" coat, as well as traits considered desirable from other popular breeds.

Therefore, in order to better understand this hybrid dog, we need to first consider the traits of all breeds involved in the careful designing of the Australian Labradoodle.

Although cross breed dogs are not recognized by purebred registries, such as the American Kennel Club (AKC), they are recognized by the International Designer Canine Registry (ICDR), where the Australian Labradoodle designer dog is generally considered to be three different sizes.

When purchasing a hybrid or designer breed canine, you need to keep in mind that while purebred dogs have been carefully bred for many generations to be recognizable by their consistently uniform look, size and temperament, puppies that are produced from combining one or more breeds, such as in the case of Australian Labradoodle, may not inherit the same consistent traits from the breeding parents.

No matter the DNA combination, the Australian Labradoodle will be a highly energy, and intelligent dog who will love to run and play and will excel at whatever activity their guardian has the time to teach.

## 1. Labrador Retriever

The large breed Labrador Retriever (Labrador or Lab) is the most popular dog worldwide, having held the American Kennel Club most popular dog breed record for 23 years in a row. Originally named the St. John's Water Dog, this dog was originally a working dog that was used to retrieve fishing nets.

This dog became a hunting and waterfowl retrieving purebred gun dog with a long history and was renamed the Labrador Retriever (after the Labrador Sea in Newfoundland, Canada) when they were first imported to England.

Apparently the Earl of Malmesbury was so impressed with this dog's skill at retrieving anything in the water that once importing several dogs, he then devoted his entire kennel to stabilizing and further developing the Labrador Retriever breed.

Development of the modern Labrador Retriever is attributed to breeding practices of many dedicated Earls, Dukes and Lords who further developed this dog for duck hunting purposes on their estates during $19^{th}$ century England, with the first Canadian dog believed to have arrived in England during 1820.

Approved breed colors are black, yellow or chocolate with a sturdy, muscular body, long, broad tail, long ears, webbed toes and a water-resistant coat for superior swimming and keeping warm in cold water. Interestingly, puppies of all three colors can appear in one litter.

The Labrador Retriever coat is short and straight and while they will shed heavily twice a year, they will also shed all year round. This dog tends to have a distinctly "doggy" smell about them.

A Labrador Retriever stands between 21½ and 24½ inches (54.6 and 62.2 centimeters) at the shoulder and can weigh between 55 and 80 pounds (24 and 36 kilograms).

The water-loving Lab is athletic, energetic, playful and most usually friendly to everyone, including all ages of children.

The enthusiastic Labrador Retriever also has a superior sense of smell, which is why they are often used as detection dogs for hunting down drug smugglers or explosives, among other things.

This dog is often seen working as a service dog for the blind or hard of hearing or in other areas of service or therapy.

The American Kennel Club (AKC) recognized the Labrador Retriever as a registered breed during 1917, and the Labrador was recognized as an official purebred canine in the United Kingdom in the year1903.

While the Labrador Retriever is an extremely enthusiastic, intelligent, easy to train dog with a large personality, that can be high energy, they are also gentle around children and older people.

This is a highly alert and enthusiastic dog that enjoys activity of any sort and can excel in canine sports such as Agility and Obedience, Flyball, Water Retrieving or Dock Diving.

When combined with their naturally active nature, this furry companion will require plenty of physical to prevent them from becoming obese, as well as continued mental stimulation, involving long walks, runs or swimming, as well as games and other types of training so that they do not become bored and develop unwanted behaviors, such as chewing anything they can find.

The Labrador Retriever has a reputation for being always hungry and it's strong sense of smell will alert this dog to any potential food source, edible or otherwise. Conscientious guardians will need to carefully oversee the feed bowl and exactly what this dog puts in its mouth to ensure that Labrador does not become overweight.

The Labrador Retriever is a friend to all with enough energy and enthusiasm to run and play fetch or swim for hours every day. If this intelligent dog does not receive plenty of daily exercise, beyond just a sedate walk around the block, they will become overweight, and extremely bored, which can lead to destructive behavior.

This is a dog that is eager to please and although rambunctious, when training begins early in their life, will be easy to train. As a result of their boundless energy and their larger size, they are not a good choice for living in an apartment or smaller living space because they tend to knock things over with their excited clumsiness and strong, whipping tail when in confined spaces.

This is a dog that needs wide-open spaces where they can run, play and fetch. The Lab will love to go running or jogging and hiking with their guardians and if there is a body of water nearby, you will have difficulty keeping them out of it.

## 2. Curly Coated Retriever

This purebred canine was originally bred in England as a bird and waterfowl retrieving dog.

The Curly Coated Retriever is one of the first of two recognized retrievers, alongside the Flat Coated Retriever, and is easily recognized by its tall stature and their very tightly curled hair. These two retriever breeds have a longstanding history that goes back to the 1860's.

This unusual retriever was the first dog bred specifically for the purpose of retrieving downed game from land or water and carrying it back to the hunter.

It is believed that the Curly Coated Retriever was developed from a combination of several breeds, including the English and Irish Water Spaniels, the St. John's Newfoundland and the Poodle.

The Curly Coated Retriever is a natural hunter that stands between 23 and 27 inches (58.4 and 69 cm) when measured at the top of the shoulder and weighs between 65 and 80 pounds (29 and 36 kilograms).

This fun-loving dog, also known as a *"Curly"* is still trained as a working gun dog hunting companion in many countries where they are highly valued as both working canines and family members.

This is a highly intelligent, loyal and affectionate dog that may get bored with repetitive training and requires plenty of daily exercise so that they can be calm family dogs in the home.

This friendly retriever gets along well with other dogs and will happily play with children for hours on end.
The Curly has an oily, single coat of very small, tight curls that is black or liver colored and that will shed minimally, which makes their coat low maintenance.

## 3. Irish Water Spaniel

The liver colored Irish Water Spaniel, native to Ireland, is one of the oldest, more rare purebred spaniels that is also the largest of the spaniels.

This water-loving dog has a non, or very low shedding, densely curled coat that has an unusually distinctive purple hue. This breed has several unusual traits, including a rat-like, smooth haired tail, an entirely smooth face that never needs trimming and a topknot of curls that often covers the dog's eyes.

The active, energetic, eager to please Irish Water Spaniel stands between 22 and 24 inches (56 and 61 centimeters), when measured at the top of the shoulder and weighs between 55 and 65 pounds (25 and 30 kilograms).

Although the Irish Water Spaniel can be wary of strangers, and has a deep bark, which makes them good watchdogs, they are usually good with children so long as they are respectful and will get along with other pets if they have been well socialized.

This spaniel has an intelligent and clownish nature, which makes fun family dogs that are easy to train

## 4. American & English Cocker Spaniels

The American Cocker Spaniel has a shorter back and is smaller than the English Cocker with a shorter muzzle and a more domed head.

The Cocker Spaniel was first bred as a hunting dog in the UK where they were named after their superior ability in hunting the Eurasian Woodcock, which is a medium-sized wading bird with a long probing beak.

The English Cocker Spaniel is taller than the American Cocker with a narrower head and chest.

While both are called Cocker Spaniels, when the breed was brought to the United States in the early part of the 20th century, several physical changes were bred into the American Cocker to help the breed excel at hunting the American Woodcock, which is a smaller shore bird.
Now, while both are closely related and both are called Cockers, the appearance between the American and the English Cocker Spaniel is distinctly different, and for the purposes of this book,

we will be referring to the American Cocker Spaniel, with their smaller size, and a shorter muzzle and rounder eyes that sets them apart from their English cousins.

While the first spaniel arrived in the United States aboard the Mayflower in the year 1620, it was not until 1878 that this medium-sized dog was registered with the American Kennel Club, with the slightly larger English Cocker Spaniel being recognized as a breed separate from the American Cocker Spaniel in 1946.

The Cocker Spaniel, smallest of the sporting class of dogs, remains popular worldwide, ranking #29 out of 177 registered American Kennel Club breeds in 2013.

While perhaps the most readily recognized breed color is the buff colored Cocker Spaniel, approved breed colors are many, including black, black and white, black, white and tan, blue roan, tan and blue roan, brown, brown and tan, brown and white, brown, cream, buff, buff and white, golden, red, red and white, red roan, sable, sable and white, silver, and white and tan.

This dog is built for speed and endurance, with a sturdy, compact body, short tail, long ears, and silky medium long length flat coat.

The Cocker Spaniel coat will moderately shed and they will require regular brushing at least several times every week, as well as clipping or trimming every few months, in order to keep their coats in good condition and free of mats and debris.

This is a sensitive dog that will usually have a distinctively "doggy" smell about them and if not trained properly may suffer from separation anxiety, which can lead to them becoming loud barkers.

This is a dog that is eager and willing to be trained and must never be treated harshly as they may become very nervous and

frightened which can cause them to act defensively and fight back.
A Cocker Spaniel stands between 13.5 and 15.5 inches (34 and 39 centimeters) at the shoulder and can weigh on average between 24 and 30 pounds (11 and 14 kilograms).

The water-loving Cocker Spaniel is athletic, energetic, playful and most usually friendly to everyone, including all ages of children.

While the Cocker Spaniel is an extremely enthusiastic, intelligent, easy to train dog with a large personality, that can be high energy, they are usually gentle around children and older people.

This is a highly alert and enthusiastic dog that enjoys activity of any sort and can excel in canine sports such as Agility and Obedience, Flyball, Water Retrieving or Dock Diving.

When combined with their naturally active nature, this furry companion will require plenty of physical to prevent them from becoming overweight, as well as continued mental stimulation, involving long walks, runs or swimming, as well as games and other types of training so that they do not become bored and develop unwanted behaviors, such as chewing anything they can find or barking and whining.

The Cocker Spaniel is a friend to all with enough energy and enthusiasm to run and play fetch or swim for hours every day.

If this intelligent dog does not receive plenty of daily exercise, beyond just a sedate walk around the block, they will become overweight, and extremely bored, which can lead to destructive behavior.

This is a dog that is eager to please and although rambunctious, when training begins early in their life, will be easy to train.
This is a dog that will love to go running or jogging and hiking with their guardians and if there is a body of water nearby, you will have difficulty keeping them out of it.

## 5. Poodle

The friendly, intelligent and active Poodle is one of the smartest dogs in the canine purebred lineup.

This fun loving canine was originally a working dog bred and developed in both Germany and Russia for field hunting which involved retrieving downed waterfowl in the water.

While still other claims of Poodle origin have been attributed to Denmark and the ancient Piedmont in Northern Mesopotamia, one thing that is certain is that today's modern Poodle was a descendant of the now-extinct French Water Dog, the Barbet, and possibly the Hungarian Water Hound.

The Poodle is believed to be one of the oldest hunting breeds used for water retrieval.

The reason the breed is referred to as the *"French Poodle"* is because the breed was standardized in France where it then became the national dog of France.

What many people don't realize is that the Poodle has been well known for very much longer than 400 or 500 years and may be one of the oldest breeds of canines known to man.
The ancient ancestral Poodle with the *"Lion Trim"* haircut appeared on ancient Greek and Roman coins during the time of

Emperor Augustus in approximately 30 A.D.

As well, the Poodle was revered in pictures that were carved on many monuments, tombs and Palace walls and there is historic evidence of the intelligent Poodle seen in medieval manuscripts of the 15th, 16th and 17th centuries.

As the Poodle became well known as a distinct breed, they were bred down in size to become more of a companion dog, which resulted in the creation of the Miniature and Toy sizes of the breed.

Poodles have been used for a variety of jobs in history as hunters and retrievers, circus dogs, court and companion dogs for the rich and powerful. The Miniature Poodle was often used as a truffle dog for sniffing out the truffle used in French gourmet cooking.

Despite the Poodle's origins as a hunting and retrieving breed, they became well known for their abilities as performing dogs, and were widely distributed due largely to traveling gypsies who favored the Poodle above all others as a performing circus dog.

As a working retriever, the Poodle was originally considered an *"off-square"* breed, because their body was longer than it was tall, which is similar to most of today's retrieving breeds.

However, as the highly intelligent Poodle was such a superior circus act performer, which made them ever more popular with the traveling gypsies, with careful breeding practices, their body shape began to change to increase their ability for faster agility which was not possible with the longer retriever body shape.

As a result, the original, longer Poodle body became more of a square shape to improve the dogs' spinning and hind leg acrobatic capabilities.

The three sizes of recognized American Kennel Club (AKC) Poodle breeds (toy, miniature and standard), rather than being judged by weight, are instead judged by height.

The toy Poodle usually stands less than 11 inches (28 centimeters) and weighs between 6 and 9 pounds (3 and 4 kilograms).

The miniature Poodle generally weighs between 15 and 17 pounds (7 to 8 kilograms) and stands between 11 and 15 inches (28 to 38 centimeters) when measured at the withers (top of the shoulder).

The miniature Poodle must be over 10 inches and 15 inches or less at the highest point of the shoulder in order to compete in the show ring as a miniature Poodle.

The standard Poodle generally stands over 15 inches (over 38 centimeters) at the shoulder and weighs between 45 and 70 pounds (20 and 32 kilograms).

Statistics indicate that according to American Kennel Club registrations, the popular Poodle continues to rank highly in popularity, holding the #9 position amongst the top 10 out of 177 registered breeds.

## 6. History/Origin of the Australian Labradoodle

While determining true origin of a specific breed of canine is always met with a certain degree of controversy and many different theories about the true origin of a breed, it is fairly clear that the first pairing of the Labrador Retriever with the Poodle took place in Australia.

In 1988 an Australia breeder (Wally Conron) paired the Labrador Retriever with the Standard Poodle in an effort to combine the trainability of the Labrador with the non-shedding coat qualities of the Poodle to create a guide dog for the blind that would not cause allergic reactions for people who are allergic to other breeds of canines.

Since this very successful first pairing in 1988, the Australian Labradoodle hybrid canine has become very popular around the world, as these dogs are not just popular family dogs, they are also used in many training programs as guide, assistance and therapy dogs.

The creation of the Australian Labradoodle is the result of more than 35 years of selective breeding, involving highly selective breeding programs in order to incorporate the desired qualities of the many purebred canines that create today's Aussie Labradoodle.

This lengthy research and development has led not just creating the perfect family canine, it has also created a wonderful service dog for the physically challenged.

The Australian Labradoodle has been carefully bred to be a loving, affectionate and sweet natured family dog inside the home, that will follow you everywhere, and also be an energetic companion ready to fully embrace any sort of canine or human/canine exercise program you may care to engage in.

There is no doubt that the melding of the very popular Labrador Retriever with the genes of the distinguished lineup of five specifically chosen purebred canines has produced a friendly, energetic and highly intelligent dog that will enjoy plenty of daily exercise.

## 7. Australian Labradoodle Secrets

Even though the Australian Labradoodle is well on its way to being recognized as a breed unto itself, created from a blending of at least six separate purebred canines, the original name of *"Labradoodle"* is a meshing together of the *"Labrad"* of the Labrador Retriever breed with the *"oodle"* of the Poodle breed to make up this hybrid dog name.

While the original Labradoodle was a Labrador Retriever bred to a Standard Poodle, just like the Poodle, who is recognized for three different sizes (Standard, Miniature and Toy) the Australian Labradoodle has also been bred in smaller sizes.

There are now three distinctly different sizes of Australian Labradoodles, including Standard, Medium or Miniature. Sizes can now range between 14 and 22 inches (35.5 and 55.8 centimeters).

The Australian Labradoodle is also known as the *"Cobberdog" or "Australian Cobber Dog",* which is an old Australian term meaning "best mate" or "friend".

The Australian Labradoodle is also known as the "Australian Service Dog" and they also make great medic alert or therapy dogs.

Please understand that much of the content written in this book can be applied to EVERY dog, because when it comes right down to it, a dog is a dog no matter what size, shape, colour, price tag or fancy hybrid name we humans might attribute to them.

Every dog has a uniquely wonderful set of gifts to share with their human counterparts, if only us humans would listen.

They "tell" us when they are unhappy, when they are bored, when they are under-exercised, yet often we do not pay attention, or we just think they are being badly behaved.

Many humans today are deciding to have dogs, instead of children, and then attempting to manipulate their dogs into being small (or large) fur children. This is having a seriously detrimental effect upon the health and behaviour of our canine companions.

In order to be the best guardians for our dogs, we humans need to have a better understanding of what our dogs need from us, rather than what we need from them, so that they can live in safety and harmony within our human environment.

Sadly, many of us humans are not well equipped to give our dogs what they really need and that is why there are so many homeless, abandoned and frustrated dogs.

As a professional dog whisperer who is challenged with the task of finding amicable solutions for canine/human relationships that have gone bad, once the humans understand what needs to be changed, almost every stressful canine/human relationship can be turned into a happy, forever after.

The sad part is that many humans are simply not willing to do the work and devote the time necessary to ensuring that their dog's needs are met.

Almost all canine problems are a direct result of ignorance or unwillingness on the part of the canine guardian to learn what the dog truly needs. Forget about the breed for the moment, because what the dog needs to be a happy and well-balanced family member has nothing to do with size, shape, colour or breed.

First and foremost, our dogs need to be respected for their unique canine qualities.

For millennia, dog has been considered *"Man's best friend",* and in today's society, when we want to do the best by our canine companions and create a harmonious relationship, we humans need to spend more time receiving the proper training so that we humans can learn how Man can be dog's best friend.

An Australian Labradoodle is a dog and therefore can be "Man's best friend" providing that the human guardian gains the knowledge they need in order to create a happy environment for the dog.

That's the biggest *"secret"* because if the human treats the dog well and understands what the dog needs, the dog will be happy and the owner will be happy. This is a universal truth that applies to any dog, whether a Australian Labradoodle or any other breed.

For example, it is not possible to write a book specifically about *"How to train a Australian Labradoodle"* or specifically about what "The first few days with your Australian Labradoodle" will entail, etc., as while basic training techniques apply to every dog, every dog and every human/dog relationship will be unique.

For this reason, when referring to daily feeding, care, house training, behavioural training, socializing, etc., these chapters are not written to apply specifically to the Australian Labradoodle breed, as this information can be applied equally successfully to any dog.

What we humans need to remember is that it is absolutely true that *"With the proper training, Man can learn to be dog's best friend."*

# Chapter 3: Breeding

## 1. Locating a Reputable Breeder

NOTE: this chapter is not about how to breed the smart and sweet-natured Australian Labradoodle, rather it is all about how to care for each stage of the dog's life.

Although a good breeder cannot guarantee the lifelong health of any puppy, they should easily be able to provide a prospective Australian Labradoodle guardian with plenty of information about the health of the puppy's parents.

Prospective guardians should definitely ask the breeder what sort of health tests have been carried out on the parents of a puppy they may be considering purchasing.

For instance, a reputable breeder will have had their breeding dogs tested for hip, thyroid, eye or other problems inherent in the breed and prospective puppy purchasers should always inquire about possible congenital problems the parents or grandparents of the puppy might have, including any premature deaths.

## 2. Meet the Parents

Meeting the mother and father of your new Australian Labradoodle puppy can tell you a great deal about what the temperament and demeanor of your puppy will likely be when they grow into adulthood.

The Australian Labradoodle puppy's personality or temperament will be a combination of what they experience in the early days of their environment when they are in the breeder's care, and the genes inherited from both parents.

Visiting the breeder several times, observing the parents, interacting with the puppies and asking plenty of questions will help you to get a true feeling for the sincerity of the breeder.

The early environment provided by the breeder and the parents of the puppies can have a formative impact on how well your puppy will ultimately behave as an adult dog.

## 3. Questions to Ask a Breeder

Get to know your breeder by asking them why they decided to breed the Australian Labradoodle and how long they have been breeding.

Ask if the breeder will permit you to visit their facility and will they give you a tour?

Ask the breeder if they own both breeding parents, or if they do not, ask if they are familiar with, or have worked closely with both parents of the Australian Labradoodle puppy you may be considering.

Ask how often the breeder allows the females and males to breed and reproduce.

Ask if the breeder will allow you to see the other dogs in the kennel and notice whether the kennel is clean, well maintained and animal friendly.

Will the breeder permit you to see other adult dogs, or other puppies that the breeder owns, socialize together?

Pay attention to whether the breeder limits the amount of time that you are permitted to handle the Australian Labradoodle puppies. A reputable breeder will be concerned for the safety and health of all their puppies and will only permit serious buyers to handle the puppies.

Check to find out if the breeder is registered or recognized by your local, state or national breed organization.

## a) Medical Questions

Every reputable breeder will certainly ensure that their Australian Labradoodle puppies have received vaccinations and de-worming specific to the age of the puppies.

Always ask the breeder what shots the puppy has received and when it was last de-wormed and ask for the name of the breeder's veterinarian.

If you discover that the breeder has not carried out any of these procedures or they are unable to tell you when the last shots or de-worming was carried out, look elsewhere.

Also ask to see the breeder's veterinarian report on the health of the puppy you may be interested in purchasing, and if they cannot produce this report, look elsewhere.

## b) Temperament Questions

You will want to choose a puppy with a friendly, easy going and congenial temperament and your breeder should be able to help you with your selection.

A good breeder will have noticed personality and temperament traits very early on in their Australian Labradoodle puppies and should be able to provide a prospective purchaser with valuable insight concerning each puppy's unique personality.

Also ask the breeder about the temperament and personalities of the puppy's parents and ask what they have done to socialize the puppies. Ask how old the puppies must be before they can be taken to their new homes. If the breeder is willing to let their puppies go any earlier than 10 weeks of age, they are more interested in making a profit than in the health of their puppies.

Always be certain to ask if an Australian Labradoodle puppy you are interested in has displayed any signs of aggression or fear, because if this is happening at such an early age, you may experience behavioral troubles when the puppy becomes older.

### c) Guarantee Questions

A reputable Australian Labradoodle breeder will be interested in the lifelong health and wellbeing of all of their puppies and good breeders will want you to call them should a problem arise at any time during the life of your Australian Labradoodle puppy.

As well, a good breeder will want you to return a puppy or dog to them, if for some reason you are unable to continue to care for it, rather than seeing the dog go to a shelter or rescue facility.

If the Australian Labradoodle breeder you are considering does not offer this type of return policy, find one who does, because no ethical breeder would ever permit a puppy from one of his or her litters to end up in a shelter.

### d) Return Contract

Reputable breeders offer return contracts. They do this to protect their reputation and to also make sure that a puppy they have sold that might display a genetic defect will not have the opportunity to breed and continue to spread the defect, which could weaken the entire breed.

Many breeders also offer return contracts because purchasing a hybrid Australian Labradoodle puppy from a breeder can be an expensive proposition, and if you find out that the puppy has a worrisome genetic defect, this could cost you a great deal with respect to unexpected veterinarian care. In such cases, most good breeders offer a return policy, and will be happy to give you another puppy.

### e) Testimonials

Ask the Australian Labradoodle breeder you are considering to provide you with testimonials from some of their previous clients, and then actually contact those people to ask them about their experience with the breeder, and the health and temperament of their Australian Labradoodle dog.

A caring, professional breeder has nothing to hide and will be more than happy to provide you with testimonials because their best recommendation is a happy customer.

### f) Breeder Reputation

The Internet can be a valuable resource when researching the reputation of an Australian Labradoodle breeder. For instance, you will be able to post on most forums discussing breeders to quickly find out what you need to know from those who have firsthand experience.

Also, be prepared to answer questions the breeder may have for you, because a reputable breeder will want to ask a prospective purchaser their own questions, so that they can satisfy themselves that you are going to be a good caretaker for their puppy.

First, do your homework about the Australian Labradoodle breed and then carry out as much research as possible about the specific breeder you are considering before making your initial visit to their facility.

The more information you have gathered about the Australian Labradoodle breed, and the breeder you are considering and the more information the breeder knows about you, the more successful the match will be.

# Chapter 4: Vital Statistics

## 1. Countries of Origin

Canada is the country of origin for the Labrador Retriever, England is the country of origin for the Curly Coated Retriever, Ireland is the country of origin for the Irish Water Spaniel, the United States is the country of origin for the American Cocker Spaniel, England is the country of origin for the English Cocker Spaniel and Germany is the country of origin for the Poodle.

In most cases with purebred canines that have been around for a very long time, it is usually very difficult to determine exactly when or who decided to first intentionally put the Labrador Retriever together with the Poodle to begin the creation of the hybrid Australian Labradoodle.

However, in the case of this carefully created breed, it is quite clear that the first pairing of these two intelligent purebreds occurred in Australia during the year 1988.

## 2. Litter Size

While more or less can be born, on average there will be 8 puppies per litter.

## 3. Height and Weight

While the Australian Labradoodle is bred in three different sizes (Standard, Medium and Miniature) these hybrid dogs can often be smaller than the Labrador Retriever parent as several of the purebred canines that make up the Australian Labradoodle breed are smaller than the Labrador Retriever, including the miniature Poodle.

There is a wide range of weights and sizes of the Poodle parent breed, therefore, when measured at the shoulder, the Australian Labradoodle may stand between 14 and 24 inches (35.5 and 60.9 centimeters) and weigh between 15 and 65 pounds (6 and 29 kilograms) depending on the size of both parents.

## 4. Temperature & Heart Rate

Temperature: 100.5 to 102.5 degrees Fahrenheit (38.05 to 39.16 Celsius).

Respiratory Rate: 10 to 20 per minute

Pulse: Puppies, 120 to 160 per minute. Adults, 60 to 140 per minute.

Gums: should be pink

## 5. Lifespan

Depending on their size, the Australian Labradoodle lifespan will be between 14 and 16 years, with some living even longer.

## 6. Intelligence

Stanley Coren, a professor of psychology at the University of British Columbia, in Vancouver, B.C., Canada, published ***The Intelligence of Dogs*** in 1994. Since then this book has become the standard for rating the particular intelligence of different canine breeds.

Coren's book describes three categories of dog intelligence:

(1) *instinctive intelligence*;

(2) *adaptive intelligence*, and

(3) *working and obedience intelligence…*

where he indicates that *"Instinctive intelligence refers to a dog's ability to carry out tasks it was bred to perform, such as guarding, herding, hunting, pointing, retrieving, or supplying companionship."* Coren further notes that:

> *"Adaptive intelligence refers to how well a dog is able to solve problems on its own.*
>
> *"Working and obedience intelligence refers to how quickly a dog is able to learn from humans."*

As the Australian Labradoodle is a combination of six purebred canines, we need to look at the intelligence of each breed separately to get an idea of what the intelligence is likely going to be for the Australian Labradoodle.

According to the findings of Stanley Coren, the Labrador Retriever ranks #7 out of a possible 79 in the *"Brightest Dogs"* category.

In other words, if one is to agree with the findings of Stanley Coren, this dog can understand new commands after less than 5 repetitions and will obey first commands 95% of the time, or better.

Stanley Coren ranks the Poodle #2 out of a possible 79, also in the *"Brightest Dogs"* category, which means that the Poodle can understand new commands after less than 5 repetitions and will obey first commands 95% of the time, or better.

Further, the Curly Coated Retriever ranks #41, the Irish Water Spaniel ranks #24, and the American and English Cocker Spaniels hold the #20 position, which means that the Australian Labradoodle will most certainly be a canine Einstein.

The Australian Labradoodle will be a highly intelligent, happy, friendly, eager and quick to learn dog that is also willing to please and easy to train.

There is no doubt that this designer dog will be an intelligent, active and happy companion that will be a wonderful family dog that also will enjoy learning new things and as much activity as their guardian can provide.

## 7. Living Conditions

The Australian Labradoodle, depending of their size, may do well in smaller living conditions, such as an apartment or condominium, while a larger dog will do better with a larger living space and a fenced yard.

No matter what size of the dog, this exuberant companion will require both mental and physical stimulation from disciplined walks and plenty of daily exercise or canine sports outside of the home.

A full grown Australian Labradoodle will need to burn off their daily pent up energy by going for at least three good walks of 30 minutes to an hour each beside their human companions every day, plus have an opportunity to run free chasing a ball or Frisbee or swimming to fetch a float or stick.

In order for this highly intelligent, happy, friendly and possibly sensitive dog to be happy and well balanced they will want to be close to their human family. This means taking your Australian Labradoodle everywhere with you, which also helps to socialize and exercise their intelligent brains.

Leaving a loving and highly intelligent dog home alone for many hours every day will be a life of boredom and torture for them that could result in the Australian Labradoodle making its own entertainment by becoming destructive and/or noisy.

# Chapter 5: Temperament

No matter which side of the extensive family tree an Australian Labradoodle puppy takes after, they are certainly going to be an energetic, fun loving, intelligent dog that lives to run and play and learn new tricks and commands.

Every dog needs the discipline of being walked on leash outside of the home each day, as well as the opportunity for off leash time to run and play fetch or enjoy socializing with other dogs.

These dogs bond strongly to humans of all ages, and truly love everyone they meet along their exciting road of life.

Most Australian Labradoodles are highly intelligent, sturdy, yet gentle dogs that are great for children of all ages. They will be loyal, alert, playful family companions that are comical, easy to train and always eager for the next adventure.

The gentle and sweet-natured Australian Labradoodle is bred to thrive on contact with humans and as a result will likely become very attached, protective and devoted to its family members.

This is not a dog that will usually be aggressive toward strangers or other dogs unless they have been coddled by their guardian and not been properly socialized at a young age.

This is an alert, intelligent, affectionate, energetic, fun-loving, clever, easy to train, eager to please dog that will be a happy family companion that will also love plenty of exercising.

If you neglect this dog and do not provide them with regular daily exercise and mental stimulation, they may decide to create their own entertainment, which could include destroying your property or barking to excess.

The Australian Labradoodle will need to be well and continually socialized at a young age, and taught to keep their boundless excitement under control.

They will be eager and interested participants that enjoy being involved in all of the family's activities, especially if they involve water or endless types of exercising.

Taking into consideration the many breeds that make up the Australian Labradoodle, this dog, as you would expect, will be an active dog that is an impressive jumper, runner and swimmer who will excel at any activity you or the family have the time to engage in.

Plenty of daily exercise will be a highly necessary part of their daily life, so that they can eliminate pent up energy, exercise their minds and their bodies and remain a healthy weight.

## 1. Behavior With Children and Pets

Generally speaking, while the Australian Labradoodle will be a good choice for active families with young children, once their puppy exuberance is under control, they will also be a good choice for families with younger children, or older adults who have the energy, time and mobility required to give them the daily exercise they need. This is a dog that can be very excitable, who really needs a structured living situation and a regular exercise routine in order to prevent anxiety and other behavioral problems that may stem from being under-exercised.

The Australian Labradoodle will usually be friendly and accepting of both unknown dogs and humans, but when not trained to live a calm life, can suffer from attachment issues with their owners.

## 2. Is This Dog an Escape Artist?

When considering the Labrador Retriever, Curly Coated Retriever, Irish Water Spaniel, American and English Spaniel and

Poodle attributes of this hybrid canine, the Australian Labradoodle will be a very athletic and talented dog with the smarts to work its way out of a confining situation to gain the freedom to run and explore, if given enough time and left alone in a yard.

As well, both the Labrador and Poodle of this hybrid cocktail are well known for their ability to scale heights and climb fences.

The Australian Labradoodle will be strongly attached to their human guardians and if they believe that they can track them down when, for instance, they have been left at home alone in a yard, they will not hesitate to figure out how to do it.

This dog should not be left alone or unsupervised outside, even in a securely fenced yard because in combination with their intelligent minds and athletic abilities, they are capable of figuring out problems, which could involve putting their strong legs to use when scaling heights no other dog would ever consider attempting.

Of course, all dogs will have a much higher urge to roam before they are spayed or neutered, therefore, early spaying or neutering of a Australian Labradoodle puppy will go a long way toward helping to curb any wanderlust tendencies that may be a result of raging hormones.

# Chapter 6: Before You Buy

## Pros and Cons

No matter what breed you may be considering as a possible candidate for sharing your home and life, this decision should never be entered into lightly.

As with any breed, those who may be considering an Australian Labradoodle need to carry out research and make sure they have all the facts straight before taking the plunge because there are always many important factors to keep in mind.

Australian Labradoodles are loving, intelligent, exuberant, active athletes who will enjoy any sort of advanced training or obedience competition, such as Agility, Rally, Dock Diving or Freestyle Dance.

This hybrid canine may also excel as a service, rescue or sniffer dog. When treated kindly and trained with positive reinforcement, the Australian Labradoodle will have a zest for learning new things very quickly and will love the attention any mental stimulation that any sort of training program provides.

If you are often away from home, this breed is not a good choice for you because this dog has been bred to be around humans, and when left alone for long periods of time may suffer from separation anxiety that will display itself by barking and destructive chewing behavior.

If expected to stay at home alone the affectionate and highly intelligent Australian Labradoodle may suffer greatly from loneliness and boredom, as they will want to always be with their guardian.This is a dog that will do well with active families with young or older children, or active seniors who prefer an energetic dog because they will be a good fit for anyone looking for a dog who is both **alert, friendly and cheerful, as well as intelligent, energetic and social.**

## 1. Pros of Australian Labradoodle Ownership

The Australian Labradoodle has many good qualities to consider, including:

- Playful, energetic and loving;
- Highly intelligent;
- Non shedding coat;
- Smaller dogs do well in apartments;
- They love to participate in canine sports;
- They live a relatively long life;
- Very eager to please and easy to train;
- Good with children of all ages;
- Good with active seniors;
- Medical alert, service and therapy dog;
- Good with other dogs and pets;
- This is an excellent choice for first time dog guardians.

## 2. Cons of Australian Labradoodle Ownership

No matter what breed you choose, there will always be some downsides to carefully consider, including:

When a hybrid becomes popular, like the Australian Labradoodle, this is all it takes for unscrupulous puppy mill breeders, who care nothing about the health or temperament of the puppies they are breeding, to get on the bandwagon.

- This can be a very active dog requiring considerable daily exercising to keep them both physically and mentally healthy;
- If not trained early in their life their exuberant personalities may make them difficult to control;
- Without the proper exercise, they can become destructive and/or difficult to handle;
- They require regular clipping;
- Not a good choice for low energy guardians as this is a high energy dog requiring plenty of daily exercise far in excess of just going out for a walk;
- Not a good dog to leave alone for long hours every day because they will literally become unhappy and bored out of their intelligent mind which can lead to destructive behavior.

# Chapter 7: Choosing the Right Dog

## 1. Where to Purchase a US Puppy

When wondering where to start your search for purchasing a Australian Labradoodle puppy in the United States, there are several clubs and registries that will be good starting points, including:

**The Australian Labradoodle Club of America** was founded in 2005 and *"was formed by the breeders of the Australian Labradoodle in America as the "Parent Club" striving toward "purebred" recognition of the breed. We are committed to protecting the health and well-being of the Australian Labradoodle by upholding the Breed Standards and maintaining the integrity of the breed as established by the breed developers in Australia.*

The American Canine Hybrid Club (ACHC) is a hybrid registry service established in 1969.

The National Hybrid Registry (NHR) is a registry service for dog's from which both parents are verified to be pure bred dogs and eligible to be registered in the National Kennel Club.

The IDCR (International Designer Canine Registry®) is considered to be a premier registry for hybrid canines around the world, with the purpose of providing hybrid or designer breed canines with certified registration and pedigree services. This Registry also provides a list of registered breeders.

**Adopt a Pet** (online): *"...is North America's largest non-profit pet adoption website. We help over 13,600 animal shelters, humane societies, SPCAs, pet rescue groups, and pet adoption agencies advertise their homeless pets to millions of adopters a* *month, for free. We're all about getting homeless pets into homes…"*

**Australian Labradoodles of Windsor Creek** (in Pennsylvania): *"We have worked very hard to become a quality breeder of Australian Labradoodle puppies and our journey continues. We are so grateful for the blessings of healthy, happy and loving Australian Labradoodle puppies going to wonderful homes and families. Our Australian Labradoodle puppy families have become cherished friends along the way and continue to keep in touch with us!"*

**Aladdin Labradoodles** (in Washington): *"…We breed our enchanting Australian Labradoodles once a year, and our Labradoodle puppies are born in our Nursery within our home in Washington State. Before our Australian Labradoodle puppies are put up for sale, we do have them de-sexed and microchipped…"*

## 2. Where to Purchase a UK Puppy

Designer Dogs – The Kennel Club is a registration and information service to help prospective owners find Kennel Club "assured breeders" of both purebreds and cross breeds.

UK Australian Labradoodle Club – "…Our aims are to educate and evangelize the public about this wonderful breed and to provide useful contacts and links for both Australian Labradoodle Breeders and prospective puppy purchasers alike…"

**Manorborn Australian Labradoodles** (in Herefordshire): *"…All Manorborn asd Australian Labradoodle puppies are born and raised in our family home. Health testing and temperaments are very important considerations with our family and you will find that our breeding stock is some of the best Australian Labradoodles that you will find…"*

**CreamofBritish Australian Labradoodles** (in Hampshire): *"CreamofBritish Australian Labradoodle breeders are not members of any Australian or UK Labradoodle Association. Our endorsement comes from owners of our puppies, many of whom have returned for a second and even a fourth puppy, we rarely advertise as most CreamofBritish puppies are homed through recommendation…"*

## 3. Average Prices for Puppies

There is a wide range of *"average"* pricing for any designer or hybrid Australian Labradoodle, with some adoptions or rescues beginning around $300 (£179).

There will be a wide variety of "average" breeder pricing for Australian Labradoodle puppies, ranging between $1,500 and $2,500 (£881 and £1,468), depending on the size of the puppies, coat and eye coloring and the expertise of the particular breeder.

Important Note: the authors of this book have not purchased dogs from all the breeders mentioned in this book, and we do not recommend any particular breeder. Make sure that you thoroughly carry out your own research before purchasing a dog from any breeder. There are many dog breeders trading purely for profit and these often will not be overly concerned about the well being of the dogs they breed.

## 4. Avoiding Puppy Mills or Farms

As soon as a particular breed of dog becomes popular, they also become particularly susceptible to being bred by disreputable, high profit *"puppy mills"* or *"commercial breeding farms"*.

Often a specific dog breed will quickly gain popularity due to the *"Lassie"* effect, which occurs when a dog is featured in a popular movie.

Puppy Mill breeding is especially prevalent with cute, smaller breeds, such as the Australian Labradoodle when bred with a toy or miniature parents.

This inhumane and cruel world of canine pregnancy for profit occurs all over the world, and if you are not very careful about where and how you purchase your Australian Labradoodle puppy, you may unknowingly end up promoting this disreputable practice.

Not only do Puppy Mills seriously contribute to overpopulation, they produce diseases, and genetically flawed puppies that may suffer greatly with behavioral and/or health related problems that will cost their guardians greatly in terms grief and stress and unexpected financial burden associated with veterinarian and behavioral costs, while the puppy's life may be cut prematurely short.

These dogs suffer in ways most of us could never imagine. For instance, most of these poor breeding dogs have never walked on solid ground or felt grass as they are housed in cramped wire cages their entire short lives.

Females are bred continuously until they can no longer produce puppies at which time they are sold to laboratories for experiments, killed or dumped on the side of a road.

Although the puppy mill problem is certainly not exclusive to the United States, as it happens all over the world, the problem is so rampant in the US that several states are actually labeled as "Puppy Mill States". These include Missouri, Nebraska, Kansas, Iowa, Arkansas, Oklahoma and Pennsylvania.

It can be difficult to shut down these mill or mass-producing farming operations because, just like the drug trade, it is business on a large and lucrative scale.

Although Puppy Mill puppies are sold in a variety of different venues, pet stores are the main source for selling these unfortunate puppies, who are taken away from their mothers far too young (at 4 to 5 weeks of age) and sold to brokers, who pack them into crates to ship them off to pet stores. Many innocent puppies die during transportation.

Think seriously before buying a puppy from a pet store because almost all puppies found in pet stores (whether or not the employees working there are aware of it) are the result of inhumane puppy mill breeding. If you purchase one of these puppies, you are helping to enable and perpetuate this horribly cruel breeding practice.

Every time someone buys a puppy from a pet store, the store will order more from the Puppy Mill. As far as the pet store is concerned, the puppies are simply inventory, like bags of dog food, and when one item drops off of the inventory list, another is purchased to replace it.

Puppy Mill puppies are also sold at flea markets, on the side of the road, at the beach, through newspaper ads and through fancy websites and Internet classifieds.

The only way to put these shameful, commercial businesses out of business is by spreading the word and never buying a puppy from a pet store, or any other advertising medium, unless you have first thoroughly checked them out by visiting the facility in person.

Always be wary if you answer an advertisement for a low priced puppy for sale and the person selling offers to deliver the puppy to you, because this could easily be the first sign that you are about to be involved in an illegal Puppy Mill operation.

Educate yourself and spread the word to others about Puppy Mills, because this is the first step toward ensuring that yourself and everyone you know are never unknowingly involved in the suffering that is forced upon the breeding dogs and puppies trapped in a puppy mill or mass farming operation.

## 5. How to Choose the Right Puppy

Choosing the <u>right</u> puppy for your family and your lifestyle is more important than you might imagine.

Many people do not give serious enough thought to sharing their home with a new puppy before they actually bring one home.

For instance, many of us choose a puppy solely based on what it looks like, because the breed may currently be popular, or because their family had the same kind of dog when they were growing up.

### a) Important Questions

In order to be fair to ourselves, our family and the puppy we choose to share our lives with, we humans need to take a serious look at our life, both as it is today and what we envision it being in the next ten to fifteen years, and then ask ourselves a few important, personal questions, and honestly answer them, before making the commitment to a puppy, including:

Do I have the time and patience necessary to devote to a puppy, which will grow into a dog who needs a great deal of attention, training and endless amounts of my devotion?

Do I lead a physically active, medium or low intensity life? For instance, am I out jogging the streets daily or climbing mountains or would I rather spend my leisure time on the couch?

Do I like to travel a lot? Perhaps a dog small enough to travel in the plane cabin with me is a consideration.

Am I a neat freak? A low or non-shedding breed, such as the Australian Labradoodle, would make more sense.

Do I have a young, growing family that takes up all my spare time and are my children old enough to carefully handle a puppy? A dog needs a lot of time and attention.

Am I physically fit and healthy enough to be out there walking a dog two to three times a day, every day, rain or shine (and much more when it's just a puppy)?

Can I afford the food costs and the veterinarian expenses that are part of being a conscientious dog guardian?

Is the decision to bring a puppy into my life a family decision, or just for the children, who will quickly lose interest?

Have I researched the breed I'm interested in, and is it compatible with my lifestyle?

What is the number one reason why I want a dog in my life?

Once you ask yourself these important questions and honestly answer them, you will have a much better understanding of the type of puppy that would be best suited for you and your family, and whether or not, it should be a Australian Labradoodle.

If you are too busy for a dog, or choose the wrong dog, you will inevitably end up with an unhappy dog, which will lead to behavioral issues, which then will lead to an unhappy family and extra expense to hire a professional to help you reverse unwanted behavioral problems. Please take the time to choose wisely.

If you have absolutely decided that the Australian Labradoodle is the right dog for you, the following tips will help you to choose the right puppy from the litter.

## b) Careful Puppy Selection

Although your breeder can often help you with selecting the right puppy for you and your family, you will likely be feeling especially drawn to one puppy over another.
Although there are other considerations, how you feel toward a particular puppy in a litter is also an important part of deciding which pup to bring home.

Beyond your feelings, considering other factors will help improve the odds of you having a positive guardianship experience with your new Australian Labradoodle puppy.

For instance, being a little objective when evaluating each puppy in the litter will help you to make the right choice.

While some people become very emotional when choosing a puppy and will be attracted to those who display extremes in behavior because they want to *"save"* them, it is not a particularly good idea to choose a puppy that may be very shy or frightened in the hope that they may grow into a happy, well-behaved dog.

Some people will delve even further into their emotional desires or needs to *"save"* or *"rescue"* and will choose a particular puppy <u>because</u> it has obvious health or behavioral issues, and because they want to provide it with a chance that they believe the puppy might not otherwise have.

While it is certainly wonderful that we humans have the capacity to raise and care for puppies that may be afflicted with health or behavior problems, it's important that these types of decisions are not undertaken lightly as such challenges can lead you down a path that could be an emotional roller coaster of highs and lows that can cause problems for both canine and human alike.

While many minor behavioral problems can be modified with early training, it's important to be aware that the time and effort needed to do so will be difficult to predict and you should be aware that *"rescuing"* a dog that could grow up to have behavioral problems may require the services of a professional dog whisperer or psychologist.

**c) Pick of the Litter**

Generally speaking, when choosing a puppy out of a litter, look for one that is friendly and outgoing, rather than one who is overly aggressive or fearful.

Taking note of a puppy's social skills, when they are still with their litter mates, will help you to choose the right puppy to take home because puppies who demonstrate good social skills with their litter mates are much more likely to develop into easy going, happy adults who play well with other dogs.

In a social setting where all the puppies can be observed together, make the following observations:

- When the puppies are playing, notice which puppies are comfortable both on top and on the bottom when play fighting and wresting with their littermates, and which puppies seem to only like being on top. Puppies who don't mind being on the bottom or who appear to be fine with either position, will usually play well with other dogs when they become adults.

- If the puppies have toys to play with, observe which puppies try to keep the toys away from the other puppies and which puppies share. Those who want to hoard the toys and keep all other puppies away may be more aggressive with other dogs over food or treats, or in play where toys are involved as they become older.

- Notice which puppies seem to like the company of the other pups and which ones seem to be loners. Puppies who like the company of their littermates are more likely to be interested in the company of other dogs as they mature than anti-social puppies.

- Observe the reaction of puppies that get yelped at when they bite or roughhouse with another puppy too hard. Puppies who ease up when another puppy yelps or cries are more likely to respond appropriately when they play too roughly as adults.

Also, check to see if the puppy you are interested in is sociable with people, because if they will not come to you, or display fear to strangers, this may be a problem when they become adults.

Further, always check if the puppy you are interested in is relaxed about being handled, because if they are not, they may become difficult with adults and children during daily interactions, during grooming or visits to the veterinarian's office.

## 6. How to Check If a Puppy is Healthy

Of course you will want to check if a puppy you are considering taking home is not just emotionally healthy, but also physically healthy.

First, ask to see veterinarian reports from the breeder to satisfy yourself that the puppy is as healthy as possible, and then once you make your decision to share your life with a particular puppy, make an appointment with your own veterinarian for a complete examination.

Before you get to this stage, however, there are a few general signs of good health to be aware of when choosing a healthy puppy from a litter, including the following:

- **Breathing** -- a healthy puppy will breathe quietly, without coughing or sneezing, and there will be no crusting or discharge around their nostrils;

- **Body** -- they will look round and well fed, with an obvious layer of fat over their rib cage;

- **Coat** – a healthy puppy will have a soft coat with no dandruff, dullness, greasiness or bald spots;

- **Energy** -- a well rested puppy will be alert and energetic;

- **Hearing** -- a healthy puppy with good hearing should react if you clap your hands behind their head;

- **Genitals** -- a healthy puppy will not have any sort of discharge visible in or around their genital or anal regions;

- **Mobility** – a healthy puppy will walk and run normally without wobbling, limping or seeming to be weak, stiff or sore; and

- **Vision**: -- a healthy puppy will have bright, clear eyes without crust or discharge and they should notice if a ball is rolled past them within their field of vision.

## 7. One Australian Labradoodle, or Two?

While getting two Australian Labradoodle puppies at once will be twice the fun, it will also be twice the work which means that you will need to be doubly alert and patient, and perhaps also lose even more sleep than you bargained for during the potty training phase.

Every puppy needs your constant attention and guidance, therefore, before taking the plunge, ask yourself if you have the time and energy to provide constant attention and guidance for two little puppies that could be running in opposite directions?

Many humans decide to get two puppies because they want their puppy to have someone to play with. Be careful that one of the reasons for this decision is not based on the fact that the human making this decision might not be the ideal candidate for having one puppy, let alone two.

For instance, if the reason you are considering two puppies is so that the one puppy will not be alone all day while you are at work, stop right there, because leaving one, two or a dozen puppies alone all day while you are at work is a terrible decision.

If this is your situation, you should NOT be considering any puppy at this stage of your life, and especially not one as loving and connected to their guardians as an Australian Labradoodle who will suffer severely by being left alone

Another consideration when thinking about whether or not to get two puppies is that often when they grow up, there may be continual sibling rivalry as each puppy vies for your attention.

It is entirely possible that when the puppies mature, they will no longer get along with each as well as they once did when they were young puppies.

Further, when you have two puppies growing up together, one will always be the more dominant personality that will take over the other, and this could mean that neither puppy will fully develop their individual personalities.

As well, when you have two puppies or dogs in your life, they generally tend to be less affectionate or interested in their human guardians as they have each other in their own pack of dogs to rely upon. This can mean that they will focus so much on each other that they will bond much less with you, which can make it more difficult to train or convince either that you are the actual leader of the pack.

Each puppy will require your individual attention when it comes time for training, and having two puppies in the picture can make it very difficult for them to concentrate or focus on the job at hand.

For instance, when you are teaching puppy #1 to “Sit” while puppy #2 is trying to bite the tail of puppy #l, your job is going to be much more challenging.

Bottom line, most professional trainers or psychologists will advise that if you want two puppies, not to get them at the exact same time, from the same litter, so that you have the opportunity to house train and teach basic commands to one puppy before you bring another one into the home.

## 8. Best Age to Purchase a Puppy

Generally speaking, no puppy, including a Australian Labradoodle puppy, should be removed from their mother any earlier than 8 weeks of age and leaving them until they are 10 to 16 weeks of age is preferred because this will give them the extra time to learn important life skills from the mother dog, including eating solid food and grooming.

As well, leaving a puppy amongst their littermates for a longer period of time will help to ensure that they learn socialization skills.

Removing a puppy from the mother and other siblings too early could mean that they will miss out on valuable skills, and may not socialize well with others.

For the first month of a puppy’s life they will be on a mother’s milk only diet. Once the puppy’s teeth begin to appear, they will start to be weaned from mother’s milk and by the age of 8 weeks should be completely weaned and eating just puppy food.

Removing a puppy from their mother any earlier than eight weeks could mean they are not fully weaned and they would be much more difficult to feed.

## 9. Should I Get a Male or Female?

Everyone you ask will have a personal opinion about whether you should get a male or a female of any breed.

While you will find just as many humans preferring a male Australian Labradoodle over a female Australian Labradoodle, if you are a first time dog guardian, there may be a few considerations that can help you to make a more informed decision.

For instance, male dogs tend to want to mark or pee on anything upright (trees, telephone poles, tall grass, a stranger's leg) wherever they are out walking much more than females, however, a dominant female will also pee on three legs in an attempt to mark territory.

A male Australian Labradoodle, even a housebroken one, may try to lift their leg on furniture when visiting a home where there are other dogs present.

When spaying and neutering your Australian Labradoodle, the operation is much more invasive when spaying a female than the neutering process required for males.

Some humans pick their dogs based on sex alone because they cannot stop themselves from attributing human characteristics to their chosen dogs, and therefore believe that, for instance, a female dog will have a *"sweeter"* temperament, or a male dog may be more *"independent"*.

Of course, this is complete nonsense, because a dog is a dog, and it can be harmful to your relationship to project human emotions onto them or imagine that they will act like humans just because we are human.

Therefore, the best way to choose your Australian Labradoodle puppy will be to take your time observing the litter when you visit the breeder.

## 10. The Australian Labradoodle Shopping List

Before bringing home your new Australian Labradoodle for the first time, there will be a list of items you need to make sure you have on hand, including:

- Food – usually the puppy will remain on whatever food they have been fed at the breeder's for at least the first couple of weeks, until they are well settled in their new home, so make sure you ask the breeder what brand to buy;

- Food and Water Bowls – make sure they are small enough for a young Australian Labradoodle puppy to get into so that they can easily eat and drink.

- Kennel – when you buy your puppy's hard-sided kennel, make sure that you buy the size that will be appropriate for them when they are full grown. It must be large enough so that (when full grown) they can easily stand up and turn around inside it;

- Soft Sided Sherpa – for easy transportation of puppies and smaller dogs. Make sure you buy the size they will need when they are full grown;

- Martingale Collar, 2 Leashes and Harness – buy the harness and collar small enough to fit your puppy and buy new collars as they grow larger.

- Leashes – you will be able to keep the same leashes as all you will ever need is a four foot (1.22 meters) leash made out of nylon webbing with a light weight clip at the end (do not buy a leash that has a heavy clip on the end as it will be difficult for your puppy to carry around;

- Soft Beds (one or two) – for them to sleep in when they are not in their kennel. Buy the beds large enough for a full grown Australian Labradoodle;

- Canine Shampoo and Conditioner;

- Finger Tooth Brush –- this is a soft rubber cap that fits over the human's finger to get the puppy used to having their teeth regularly brushed;

- Soft Bristle Brush or Comb for longer coats – for daily grooming;

- Puppy Nail Scissors – for trimming their toenails, and a medium or large-sized pair of plier style nail clippers for when they are full grown;

- One or two Soft Toys -- or wait until they come home and let them pick their own toys from the store;

- Puppy sized Treats;

- Poop Bags;

- Pee Pads;

- Bath Towels;

- Non-slip Mat for the sink or tub.

Be sure to take your Australian Labradoodle shopping list with you when you go to your local pet store or boutique, otherwise you may forget critical items.

NOTE: if you do not already have a hairdryer, you will need to get one of these, too, so you can dry your puppy after bath time.

## 11. Puppy Proofing Your Home

Most puppies will be a curious bundle of energy, eager to explore everything, which means that they will get into everything within their reach.

As a responsible puppy guardian, you will want to provide a safe environment for them, which means eliminating all sources of danger, similar to what you would do for a curious toddler.

Be aware that your Australian Labradoodle puppy will want to touch, sniff, taste, chew, investigate and closely inspect every electrical cord, every closet, every nook and cranny of your home and everything you may have left lying about on the floor.

Power cords can be found in just about every room in the home and to a teething puppy, these may look like irresistible, fun, chew toys. Make sure that you tuck all power cords securely out of your puppy's reach or enclose them inside a chew-proof PVC tube.

Kitchen – first of all, there are many human foods that can be harmful to dogs, therefore, your kitchen should always be strictly off limits to your puppy any time you are preparing food.

Calmly send them out of the kitchen any time you are in the kitchen, and they will quickly get the idea that this area is off limits to them.

Bathroom – bathroom cupboards and drawers or the side of a bathtub where you may leave your shaving supplies can hold many dangers for a young and curious Australian Labradoodle puppy.

Kleenex, cotton swabs, Q-tips, toilet paper, razors, pills, soap or other materials left within your puppy's reach are an easy target that could result in an emergency visit to your veterinarian's office.

Family members need to put shampoos, soap, facial products, makeup and accessories out of reach or safely inside a cabinet or drawer.

Bedroom – if you don't keep your shoes, slippers and clothing safely behind doors, you may find that your puppy has claimed them for their new chew toys.

Be vigilant about keeping everything in its safe place, including jewelry, hair ties, bills, coins, and other items small enough for them to swallow in containers or drawers, and secure any exposed cords or wires.

If you have children, make sure they understand that, especially while your puppy is going through their teething stage, they must keep their rooms picked up and leave nothing that could cause a choking problem to the puppy lying about on the floor or within their reach.

Living Room – we humans spend many hours in our cozy gathering places to watch movies or play games, and often the living areas of our homes will have many items that are very enticing for a curious and teething puppy, such as books, magazines, pillows, iPods, cell phones, TV remotes and more.

You will want to keep your home free of excess clutter and remain vigilant about straightening up and putting things out of sight that could be tempting to your puppy.

Office – we humans often spend a great deal of time in our home offices, which means that our puppy will want to be there, too, and they will be curious about all the items an office has to offer, such as cell phones, papers, books, magazines, and electrical cords.

Although your puppy might think that rubber bands or paper clips are fun to play with, allowing these items to be within your puppy's reach could end up being a fatal mistake if your puppy swallows them.

Plants: – can be a very tempting target for your puppy's teeth, so you will want to keep them well out their reach.
If you have floor plants, they will need to be moved to a shelf or counter or placed behind a closed door until your curious fur friend grows out of the habit of putting everything in their mouth. Also keep in mind that many common houseplants are poisonous to dogs (discussed in Chapter 16).

Garage and Yard – there are obvious as well as subtle dangers that could seriously harm or even kill an Australian Labradoodle puppy, which can often be found in the garage or yard.

Some of these might include antifreeze, gasoline, fertilizers, rat, mice, snail and slug poison, weed killer, paint, cleaners and solvents, grass seed, bark mulch and various insecticides.

If you are storing any of these toxic substances in your garage or garden shed, make certain that you keep all such products inside a locked cabinet, or stored on high shelves that your puppy will not be able to reach. Even better, choose not to use toxic chemicals anywhere in your home or yard.

## 12. Puppy Hazard Home Inspection

Every conscientious puppy guardian needs to take a serious look around the home not just from the human eye level, but also from the eye level of an Australian Labradoodle puppy.

This means literally crawling around your floors. This can be a fun exercise to ask your children to help you with.

Your puppy has a much lower vantage point than you do when standing, therefore, there may be items in your environment that could potentially be harmful to a Australian Labradoodle puppy that a human might not notice unless you get down on the floor and take a really good look.

## 13. First Weeks With Your Puppy

### a) The First Night

Before you go to the breeder's to pick up your new Australian Labradoodle puppy, vacuum your floors, including all the dust bunnies under the bed.

Do a last minute check of every room to make sure that everything that could be a puppy hazard is carefully tucked away out of sight and that nothing is left on the floor or low down on shelves where a curious puppy might get into trouble.

Close most of the doors inside your home, so that there are just one or two rooms that the puppy will have access to.

You have already been shopping and have everything you need, so get out a puppy pee pad and have it at the ready when you bring your new fur friend home.

Also have your soft bed(s) in an area where you will be spending most of your time and where your puppy can easily find them.

If you have already purchased a soft toy, take the toy with you when you go to pick up your puppy.
NOTE: take either your hard-sided kennel or your soft-sided "Sherpa" travel bag (lined with pee pads) with you when going to bring your new Australian Labradoodle puppy home, and make

sure that it is securely fastened to the seat of your vehicle with the seatbelt restraint system.

Even though you will be tempted to hold your new Australian Labradoodle puppy in your lap on the drive home, this is a very dangerous place for them to be, in case of an accident.

Place them inside their kennel or bag, which will be lined with soft towels and perhaps even a warm, towel wrapped hot water bottle (and a pee pad), and close the door.

If you have a friend who can drive for you, sit beside your puppy in the back seat, and if they cry on the way home, remind them that they are not alone with your soft, soothing voice.

Before bringing your new Australian Labradoodle puppy inside your home, take them to the place where you want them to relieve themselves and try to wait it out long enough for them to at least go pee.

Then bring them inside your home and introduce them to the area where their food and water bowls will be kept, in case they are hungry or thirsty.

Let your puppy wander around sniffing and checking out their new surroundings and encourage them to follow you wherever you go.

Show them where the puppy pee pad is located and place it near the door where you will exit to take them outside to go potty. Many pee pads are scented to encourage a puppy to pee, and if they do, happily praise them.

Show them where their hard-sided kennel is (in your bedroom) and put them inside with the door open while you sit on the floor in front and quietly encourage them to relax inside their kennel.

Depending on the time of day when you bring your new Australian Labradoodle puppy home for the first time, practice this kennel exercise several times throughout the day, and if they will take a little treat each time you encourage them to go inside their kennel, this will help to further encourage the behavior of them wanting to go inside.

After they have had their evening meal, take them outside approximately 20 minutes later to go to the bathroom, and when they do, make sure you are very enthusiastic with your praise and perhaps even give a little treat.

So far your Australian Labradoodle puppy has only been allowed in several rooms of your home, as you have kept the other doors closed, so keep it this way for the first few days.

Before it's time for bed, again take your puppy outside for a very short walk to the same place where they last went potty and make sure that they go pee before bringing them back inside.

Before bed, prepare your Australian Labradoodle puppy's hot water bottle and wrap it in a towel so that it will not be too hot for them, and place it inside their hard-sided kennel (in your bedroom).

Turn the lights down low and invite your puppy to go inside their kennel and if they seem interested, perhaps give them a soft toy to have inside with them. Let them walk into the kennel under their own steam and when they do, give them a little treat (if they are interested) and encourage them to snuggle down to sleep while you are sitting on the floor in front of the kennel.

Once they have settled down inside their kennel, close the door, go to your bed and turn all the lights off. It may help your puppy to sleep during their first night home, if you can play quiet, soothing music in the background.

If they start to cry or whine, stay calm and have compassion because this is the first time in their young life when they do not have the comfort of their mother or their litter mates.

Do not let them out of their kennel if they are crying, but rather, simply reassure them with your calm voice that they are not alone until they fall asleep.

TIP: if your bed is wide enough to accommodate your puppy's kennel, it may help them to fall asleep for the first few nights in their new kennel, if you have it beside you on top of the bed, so that you are closer to them. If there is any danger of the kennel falling off the bed during the night, do NOT do this as you will traumatize your puppy and make them afraid of their kennel.

**b) The First Week**

During the first week, you and your new Australian Labradoodle puppy will be getting settled into their new routine, which will involve you getting used to your puppy's needs as they also get used to your usual schedule.

Be as consistent as possible with your waking and sleeping routine, getting up and going to bed at the same time each day, so that it will be easier for your puppy to get into the flow and routine of their new life.

First thing in the morning, remove your puppy from their kennel and take them immediately outside to relieve themselves at the place where they last went pee.

At this time, if you are teaching them to ring a doorbell to go outside, let them ring the bell before you go out the door with them, whether you are carrying them, or whether they are walking out the door on their own.

NOTE: during the first week, you may want to carry your puppy outside first thing in the morning as they may not be able to hold it for very long once waking up.

When you bring them back inside, you can let them follow you so they get used to their new leash and/or harness arrangement.

Be very careful not to drag your puppy if they stop or pull back on the leash.

TIP: if they refuse to walk on the leash, just hold the tension toward you (without pulling) while encouraging them to walk toward you, until they start to move forward again.
Now it will be time for their first feed of the day, and after they have finished eating, keep an eye on the clock, because you will want to take them outside to relieve themselves in about 20 minutes.

When your puppy is not eating or napping, they will be wanting to explore and have little play sessions with you and these times will help you bond with your puppy more and more each day.

As their new guardian, it will be your responsibility to keep a close eye on them throughout the day, so that you can notice when they need to relieve themselves and either take them to their pee pad or take them outside.

You will also need to make sure that they are eating and drinking enough throughout the day, so set regular feeding times at least three times a day.

Also set specific times in the day when you will take your puppy out for a little walk on leash and harness, so that they are not only going outside when they need to relieve themselves, but they are also learning to explore their new neighborhood with you beside them.

When your Australian Labradoodle puppy is still very young, you will not want to walk for a long time as they will get tired easily, so keep your walks to no more than 15 or 20 minutes during your first week and if they seem tired or cold, pick them up and carry them home.

## 14. Common Mistakes to Avoid

### a) Sleeping in Your Bed

Many humans make the mistake of allowing a crying puppy to sleep with them in their bed, and while this may help to calm and comfort a new puppy, it will set a dangerous precedent that can result in behavioral problems later in their life.

As well, a sleeping human body can easily crush an Australian Labradoodle puppy.

As much as it may pull on your heart strings to hear your new Australian Labradoodle puppy crying the first couple of night in their kennel, a little tough love at the beginning will keep them safe while helping them to learn to both love and respect you as their leader.

### b) Picking Them Up at the Wrong Time

Never pick your puppy up if they display nervousness, fear or aggression (such as growling) toward an object, person or other pet, because this will be rewarding them for unbalanced behavior.

Instead, your puppy needs to be gently corrected by you, with firm and calm energy so that they learn not to react with fear or aggression.

### c) Armpit Alligators

If your Australian Labradoodle is a small size, be aware that many guardians get into the bad habit of carrying a small dog far too much. They need to be on the ground and walking on their own so that they do not become overly confident because a dog that is carried by their guardian is literally being placed in the *"top dog"* position.

Humans who constantly carry small dogs around rather than allowing them to walk on their own can often inadvertently create what I refer to as an *"armpit alligator"* situation.

While the Australian Labradoodle usually has a softer, friendly temperament that is tolerant of other people and pets, it is possible to allow them to become protective or possessive of *"their"* humans.

This happens when the dog becomes possessive of it's guardian who carries it everywhere, and when another adult, child or dog sees the cute little dog and approaches to say hello, the cute little dog who has been inadvertently trained to believe that it is the boss, may then lunge, snap and/or growl.

**d) Playing Too Hard or Too Long**

Many humans play too hard or allow their children to play too long or too roughly with a young puppy. You need to remember that a young puppy tires very easily and especially during the critical growing phases of their young life, they need their rest.

**e) Hand Play**

Always discourage your Australian Labradoodle puppy from chewing or biting your hands, or any part of your body for that matter.

If you allow them to do this when they are puppies, they will want to continue to do so when they have strong jaws and adult teeth and this is not acceptable behavior for any breed of dog.

Do not get into the habit of playing the *"hand"* game, where you rough up the puppy and slide them across the floor with your hands, because this will teach your puppy that your hands are playthings.

When your puppy is teething, they will naturally want to chew on everything within reach, and this will include you. As cute as you might think it is, this is not an acceptable behavior and you need to gently, but firmly, discourage the habit.

A light flick with a finger on the end of a puppy nose, combined with a firm "NO" and removing the enticing fingers by making a fist when they are trying to bite human fingers will discourage them from this activity.

**f) Not Getting Used to Grooming**

Not taking the time to get your Australian Labradoodle used to a regular grooming routine, including bathing, brushing, toenail clipping and teeth brushing can lead to a lifetime of trauma for both human and dog every time these procedures must be performed.

Set aside a few minutes each day for your grooming routine.

NOTE: get your Australian Labradoodle used to being up high, on a table or countertop when you are grooming them, because when it comes time for a full grooming session, then they will not be stressed by being placed on a grooming table.

**g) Free Feeding**

Free feeding means to keep food in your puppy's bowl 24/7 so that they can eat any time of the day or night, whenever they feel like it.

While free feeding a young puppy can be a good idea (especially with very small dogs) until they are about four or five months old,

many guardians often get into the bad habit of allowing their adult dogs to continue to eat food any time they want, by leaving food out 24/7.
This can be a serious mistake, as your dog needs to know that you are absolutely in control of their food.

If your Australian Labradoodle does not associate the food they eat with you, they may become picky eaters or think that they are the boss, which can lead to other behavioral issues later in life.

**h) Treating Them Like Fur Children**

Do not get into the bad habit of treating your Australian Labradoodle like a small fur human, because even though they may try their best to please you, and their doggy smarts could help them to succeed in most instances, not honoring them for the amazing dog they are will only cause them confusion that could lead to behavioral problems.

Remember that the one thing that your Australian Labradoodle is the absolute best at is being a dog.

A well-balanced Australian Labradoodle thrives on rules and boundaries, and when they understand that there is no question that you are their leader and they are your follower, they will live a contented, happy and stress-free life.

i) Distraction and Replacement

When your puppy tries to chew on your hand, foot, or your clothing, or anything else that is not fair game, you need to firmly and calmly tell them "No", and then distract them by replacing what they are not supposed to be chewing with their chew toy.

Make sure that you happily praise them every time they choose the toy to chew on.

If the puppy persists in chewing on you, remove yourself from the equation by getting up and walking away. If they are really persistent, put them inside their kennel with a favorite chew toy until they calm down.
Always praise your puppy when they stop inappropriate behavior so that they begin to understand what they can and cannot do.

## 15. Bonding With Your Dog

You will begin bonding with your Australian Labradoodle puppy from the very first moment you bring them home from the breeders.

This is the time when your puppy will be the most upset and nervous, as they will no longer have the guidance, warmth and comfort of their mother or their other littermates, and you will need to take on the role of being your new puppy's center of attention.

Be patient, kind and gentle with them as they are learning you are now their new center of the universe.

Your daily interaction with your puppy during play sessions and especially your disciplined exercises, including going for walks on leash, and teaching commands and tricks, will all be wonderful bonding opportunities.

Do not make the mistake of thinking that *"bonding"* with your new puppy can only happen if you are playing or cuddling together, because the very best bonding happens when you are kindly teaching rules and boundaries, and this intelligent puppy will be most eager to learn.

## 16. What Does the Wag Mean?

It can be a mistake to automatically assume that if a dog is wagging their tail that they are happy and friendly.

When determining a dog's true intent or demeanor, you need to take into consideration the entire dog because it is entirely possible that a dog can be wagging it's tail just before it decides to take an aggressive lunge toward you.
More important in determining the emotional state of a dog is the height or positioning of the their tail.

For instance, a tail that is held parallel to the dog's back usually suggests that the dog is feeling relaxed, whereas, if the tail is held stiffly vertical, this usually means that the dog may be feeling aggressive or dominant.

A tail held much lower can mean that the dog is feeling stressed, afraid, submissive or unwell and if the tail is tucked underneath the dog's body, this is most often a sign that the dog is feeling stressed, fearful or threatened by another dog or person.

Paying attention to your dog's tail can help you to know when you need to step in and make some space between your dog and another more dominant dog.

Of course, different breeds naturally carry their tails at different heights, so you will need to take this into consideration when studying your dog's tail so that you get used to their particular signals.

As well, the speed the tail is moving will also give you an idea of the mental state of the dog because the speed of the wag usually indicates how excited a dog may be.

For instance, a slow, slightly swinging wag can often mean that the dog is tentative about greeting another dog, and this is more of a questioning type of wag, whereas a fast moving tail held high can mean that a dog is about to challenge or threaten another less dominant dog.

Interestingly, two veterinarians at the University of Bari and a neuroscientist at the University of Trieste, in Italy, published a paper in which their research outlined that dogs' tails wagged more to their right side when they had positive feelings about a person or situation, and more to the left side when they were feeling negative.

While certainly a dog's tail can help us humans to understand how our dogs might be feeling, there are many other factors to take into consideration when determining your dog's state of mind.

## 17. What Does the Bark Mean?

Of course, our dogs bark for a wide variety of reasons, and every dog is different, depending upon their natural breed tendencies and how they were raised, and this section discusses some of the more common reasons why a dog might be barking.

### a) Communication

Since the very first dog, they have communicated over long distances by howling to one another and when in closer proximity, barking to warn off other dogs approaching what they consider to be their territory or in excitement or happiness when greeting another member of the dog pack.

Now, our domesticated dogs have learned that barking for a wide variety of reasons, in a guard dog capacity to alert us to someone approaching the home, in anticipation of their favorite food, when they are afraid or frustrated, or to let us know they want to play is an effective way to get the attention of us humans because barking is a difficult noise to ignore.

### b) Danger

Of course, our canine companions will bark to alert us to what they believe might be a dangerous situation, but how do we learn to understand the difference between what our dogs perceive as danger and what is truly dangerous, or indeed teach our best friends the difference?

We want our dogs to tell us when there is a real imminent danger and in this case, should the danger involve an unwanted intruder, we want them to bark loudly to possibly scare this threat away.

Unfortunately, many dogs are not quite as discerning as we humans might prefer, and as such they may end up barking during situations that we humans would consider inappropriate or just plain annoying.

When our dogs are barking for a reason we are not yet aware of, we need to calmly assess the situation rather than immediately becoming annoyed. We also need to remember that our dog's sense of smell, hearing and sometimes eyesight is far more acute than our own, so we need to give them an opportunity to tell us they just heard, saw or sensed something that they are worried or uncertain about.

Rather than ignoring our dogs (or yelling at them) when they are attempting to "tell" us that something is bothering them, even if we ourselves understand that the noise the dog just heard is only the neighbor pulling into their driveway, is to calmly acknowledge the dog's concern by saying, *"OK, good boy"* or *"OK, good girl"* and then asking them to come to you. This way you have quietly and calmly let your dog know that the situation is nothing to be concerned about and you have asked them to move away from the target they are concerned about, which will usually stop the barking.

### c) Attention

Many dogs will learn to bark to get their owner's attention, just because they are bored or want to be taken outside for an interesting walk or a trip to the local park to chase a ball.

Our canine companions are very good at manipulating us in this way, and if we fall for it, we are setting up an annoying precedent that could plague us for the remainder of our relationship.

When a dog is barking to gain their guardian's attention, even if it is warranted because (in this example) it is certainly time to go out for a walk, we humans must not be immediately manipulated. Instead, we need to calmly ask our dog to do something for us, before leaping up and getting the leash to take our dog out.

After our dog has performed a calm and quiet task for us, such as sit and lie down, then we can decide to take our dog out for a walk.

In another example, often you will see a dog and their guardian at the local dog park playing fetch and when the human is not throwing that ball quickly enough to satisfy the dog's desire to run and fetch, the dog will be madly barking at the human guardian.

Do not make the mistake of allowing your dog to manipulate you in this situation, because if you do, you will have created another bad habit that will very quickly become not just annoying to you, but also annoying to everyone else in the park.

Before throwing a ball or Frisbee, etc., for a dog that loves to retrieve, it is important to always ask the dog to sit and make eye contact with you.

Often the types of canines that are overly exuberant with chasing a ball or Frisbee have learned this barking behavior from their humans who allowed themselves to be literally at the beckon call of the dog, and they did this by throwing the ball every time the dog barked.

If you allow your dog to dictate to you when you will throw the ball, they will quickly learn that barking gets them their desired result, and you have just created an annoying, rude dog who is yelling at you in doggy language to do their bidding.

In this type of ball retrieving scenario, the dog has become ball *"obsessed"* and is no longer really paying attention to the guardian's commands, as they are solely focusing on where the ball is.

There are many situations in which a dog may bark to convey a certain message, such as letting you know when they need to go outside for potty, and of course, this is a good thing.

However, in all other situations where a dog is barking to demand attention or an object or food, this is when you need to ask them to do something for you, and then only if you want to give them what they are asking for, do you follow through.

Also, remember to stay calm when a dog is demanding attention because even negative attention can be rewarding for a dog that can then learn further habits that will not be particularly acceptable for the human side of the relationship.

## d) Boredom or Separation Anxiety

Many dogs, especially those who have not been properly trained or that have not been allowed to understand that they have rules and boundaries, and are treated like children, will bark loudly when left at home alone and they are bored or are feeling the anxiety of being alone.

Many times we humans believe that a dog is barking when being left alone because the dog is experiencing "separation anxiety", when in fact what the dog is really experiencing is the frustration of observing a member of the pack which they believe to be their follower (i.e. You) leaving them and they are loudly verbalizing this frustration and displeasure that the pack follower does NOT leave the pack leader.

In these cases, the humans really need the expert advice of a dog whisperer or dog psychologist to help turn the situation around and put the human guardian back in the driver's seat.

Breaking a dog of the habit of loud barking when they are left alone can be solved in two different ways.

The most obvious being that you simply take your dog with you wherever you go, because after all, they are pack animals, and in order for them to be really happy and well balanced, they need the constant direction of their leader (which is supposed to be you).

The other, much more lengthy and often more time consuming way to solve a barking problem, involves hiring a professional to help assess why the problem has occurred and devise a plan that will work for your unique situation.

## e) Fear or Pain

Another reason our canine companions will bark is when they are very frightened or in pain and this is usually a type of bark that sounds quite different from all the others, often being a combination of a bark and a whine, or a yelping type of noise.

This is a bark that you will want to pay close attention to so that you can quickly respond and offer the dog assistance that they may need.

Whatever reason your dog may be barking, always remember that this is how they communicate and "tell" us that they want something or are concerned, afraid, nervous or unhappy about something, and as their guardians, we humans need to pay attention.

# Chapter 8: Health Problems

When considering what sort of health problems a designer or cross bred dog may be prone to, you will need to first consider the health problems associated with each breed individually.

Next, you will need to take into consideration that if the designer dog is 50% one breed and 50% another that this crossing will provide the puppies with the benefits of what is called “hybrid vigor”.

This means that a hybrid puppy will likely benefit physically as well as mentally from having a more varied genetic makeup than a 100% purebred puppy which could be afflicted by or susceptible to health problems that both of the purebred parents may also have.

## 1. Labrador Retriever

While a healthy Labrador Retriever is not generally plagued with many health problems and may live on average 10 to 12 years or longer, common genetic and other health problems that may afflict a Labrador Retriever include:

### a) Hip and Elbow Dysplasia

This is a condition in which the head of the femur fits improperly into the hip or elbow joint socket. Factors that have an influence include nutrition, as this is a dog that suffers from obesity, a dog's environment and the condition of the hips of its parents. Screening for hip dysplasia is recommended for breeding stock.

### b) Luxating Patella

This slipping kneecap condition is a common defect seen in many breeds, including the Labrador Retriever, that may also be caused by accidentally falling or jumping from a height.

Often you will see a dog with this problem appear to be skipping down the road as they occasionally life one leg when the kneecap slips out of the patellar groove and the leg locks up.

Surgery is the treatment option for this condition, although many dogs live a relatively normal life with this defect.

**c) Progressive Retinal Atrophy**

Some Labrador Retrievers can suffer from several eye problems, including Progressive Retinal Atrophy (PRA). PRA causes degeneration of the retina, which is part of the eye. The retina is the part that senses visual information and sends it to the brain.

Degeneration of this vital part of the eye eventually will lead to blindness. ) This disease usually appears between 3 and 5 years of age. A simple DNA test is available to determine (without waiting for symptoms to appear).

**d) Cataracts**

Cataracts (which are common in many breeds), is an eye condition where the lens becomes cloudy or milky, which would be like trying to see through a foggy window. This eye condition can appear from birth to 3 years of age and will usually lead to blindness.

**e) Corneal Dystrophy**

This disease is a change in the eye usually attributed to aging, causing fluid leakage that appears as a bluish color in the inner layer of the cornea.

**f) Retinal Dysplasia**

This eye disease appears as streaks or dots in the retina of the dog's eye, which can lead to blindness.

**g) Hereditary Myopathy**

This is a disease of the muscles that causes weakness in the muscle tissues when the fibers of the muscles cease to function. This condition is usually considered to eventually be lethal with the cause often being cited as stress or over exertion of the muscles. Symptoms can include a shortened gait often referred to as *"bunny hopping"*.

**h) Exercise Induced Collapse**

Exercise Induced Collapse (EIC) usually appears following short periods of strenuous exercise and can display as disorientation, weakness, collapse and hyperthermia.

Labradors affected with this syndrome often are able to tolerate mild or moderate exercise, however, a short period (5 to 20 minutes) of excitement or strenuous activity, which often occurs during hunting tests or field trials, can cause weakness leading to collapse. Dogs with this syndrome can live normal lives so long as they do not continue with intense training routines.

**i) Obesity**

Many Labradors are overweight, simply because they love to eat and when love of eating is combined with little or no exercise, which then leads to laziness, much like us humans, they will easily become obese.

While obesity is a serious condition that plagues many breeds of dogs, the Labrador seems to be more prone to this health problem.

Many noted health conditions can be prevented when conscientious breeders carefully screen breeding stock so that hereditary or genetic health conditions will not be passed on to subsequent litters of puppies.

## 2. Curly Coated Retriever

### a) Hip Dysplasia

This is a condition in which the head of the femur fits improperly into the hip joint socket. Factors that have an influence include nutrition, as this is a dog that suffers from obesity, a dog's environment and the condition of the hips of its parents. Screening for hip dysplasia is recommended for breeding stock.

### b) Epilepsy

Seizures can occur in all three sizes of Poodle and the most common cause is idiopathic epilepsy, which is an inherited form of epilepsy.

However, many factors can cause seizures and it is very important to have a Miniature Poodle diagnosed if seizures begin.

### c) Heart Disease

This breed can suffer from genetic subaortic stenosis (SAS), which is the second most commonly inherited heart disease in dogs usually discovered when the puppy is young and being examined by the veterinarian who hears an unusual heart murmur.

In the case of subaortic stenosis the puppy will be born with a narrowed passage leading from the aorta to the heart and if the passage continues to narrow, blood flow will become more and more restricted, often leading to sudden death.

Treatment may involve drugs to reduce heart rate and lower blood pressure. Surgery can be performed, however, open heart surgery is extremely invasive and the results tend to be similar to those dogs that receive drug treatment.

This breed also suffers from patent ductus arteriosus (PDA), which is the most common heart disease found in dogs, and compared to the heart murmur sound of SAS, will sound more like a washing machine.

After a puppy is born and the lungs expand, the connection between the puppy's pulmonary artery (ductus arteriosus) and the aorta is supposed to naturally close. If it does not close and stays open (called patent) blood is then shunted through the artery from the high-pressure aorta to the low-pressure pulmonary artery, resulting in an excessive blood flow to the lungs.

A puppy suffering from PDA may seem normal for the first few weeks of its life, other than being the smallest in the litter and appearing to become tired more easily when playing. When examined by the vet, they will hear a loud, continuous murmur.

Early treatment to surgically correct the defect, around 2-3 months of age, is important if the puppy is going to survive. Sadly, without surgery approximately 60% will die within one year. When completed early, surgery for this heart problem is very successful with a 90% survival rate and an excellent prognosis for leading a normal life.

**d) Pyoderma**

This is a bacterial infection of the dog's skin that causes itching and redness that can lead to lesions on the skin that are similar to pimples. Treatment involves shampoo and antibiotic creams.

**e) Follicular Dysplasia**

This is a genetic condition that causes hair loss due to structural abnormality or weakened hair follicles, which can also be caused by injury or excessive grooming. There is no cure and this more commonly occurs on the back of the dog, near the tail.

**f) Cataracts**

Cataracts usually appear between the ages of two and four years and are common in many breeds. This is an eye condition where the lens becomes cloudy or milky, which would be like trying to see through a foggy window. This eye condition can appear from birth to 3 years of age and will usually lead to blindness.

**g) Entropion**

This is a condition in which the dog's eyelid will roll inward which then causes the lashes to rub against the eyeball. Left untreated, this condition can severely damage the dog's eye, even causing blindness. Surgery is required to correct this problem.

**h) Ectropion**

In a dog suffering from this condition the lower eyelid will turn outward and requires surgery to repair.

**i) Corneal Dystrophy**

This disease is a change in the eye usually attributed to aging, causing fluid leakage that appears as a bluish color in the inner layer of the cornea.

**j) Retinal Dysplasia**

This eye disease appears as streaks or dots in the retina of the dog's eye, which can lead to blindness.

**k) Persistent Pupillary Membranes**

As the name suggests, this is a condition that occurs when remaining blood vessels that were necessary for supplying nutrients to the puppy's eyes before birth persist or remain in the dog's eye as strands of tissue, rather than disappearing around the age of 4 to 5 weeks.

Thankfully, as there is no treatment, this problem causes little problem unless the remaining tissue becomes attached to the lens or cornea of the dog's eye. If this should happen, vision may be compromised.

**l) Progressive Retinal Atrophy**

PRA causes degeneration of the retina, which is part of the eye. The retina is the part that senses visual information and sends it to the brain.

Degeneration of this vital part of the eye eventually will lead to blindness. ) This disease usually appears between 3 and 5 years of age. A simple DNA test is available to determine (without waiting for symptoms to appear).

**m) Bloat**

Bloat is a life-threatening, common occurrence that can affect any deep-chested canine, such as the Chow. 50% of dogs that develop bloat do not survive. This condition can happen very quickly, especially if you feed your dog right after vigorous exercise, or if they are a very fast eater and gulp in large quantities of air with their food.

The stomach then distends with gas and fluid which can cause the stomach to twist 180-degrees or more. When the stomach is closed off, the food is then trapped inside where it will ferment and cause the stomach to bulge. The bulging stomach can then interfere with blood circulation. Bloat is a serious, life-threatening condition that requires immediate veterinary intervention. If you have a deep chested dog that tends to gulp their food, get them a slow feeder type of bowl to slow down their eating process and never feed them immediately after exercise or having had a large drink of water.

**n) Hypothyroidism**

This is a condition resulting from an inadequate production of thyroid hormone which is treated with medication. Symptoms can include weight gain or obesity, constant hunger, reduced energy and a coarser the feel of the dog's coat texture. Blood samples will be taken in order to test for a malfunctioning thyroid.

### o) Osteochondritis

This is a joint disorder that causes cracks to form in the cartilage and underlying bone and is caused by lack of blood flow to the cartilage, which then results in the bone dying and being absorbed by the dog's body. When this occurs the joint can no longer move freely and movement causes discomfort, pain and more damage.

Causes of Osteochondritis can be due to trauma, poor nutrition, genetics or improper or too strenuous exercising at an early age and can affect the shoulder, knee, elbow or hock joints.

Diagnosis required x-ray and restricted activity. In severe cases surgery will be required to remove the defective cartilage.

### p) Von Willebrand Disease

This is a blood disorder similar to hemophilia in humans where blood does not clot properly, which means that if the dog becomes injured, they are more likely to suffer from excessive bleeding episodes.

There is a simple DNA test available to rule out this disease at any time, rather than waiting for symptoms to appear.

## 3. Irish Water Spaniel

### a) Hip and Elbow Dysplasia

This is a condition in which the head of the femur fits improperly into the hip or elbow joint socket. Factors that have an influence include nutrition, as this is a dog that suffers from obesity, a dog's environment and the condition of the hips of its parents.

Screening for hip dysplasia is recommended for breeding stock.

**b) Pyoderma**

This is a bacterial infection of the dog's skin that causes itching and redness that can lead to lesions on the skin that are similar to pimples. Treatment involves shampoo and antibiotic creams.

**c) Nail Bed Disease**

Dog nails may suffer from infection or trauma and a nail deformity may be caused by a number of diseases, the cause of which is often unknown and incurable.

**d) Follicular Dysplasia**

This is a genetic condition that causes hair loss due to structural abnormality or weakened hair follicles, which can also be caused by injury or excessive grooming. There is no cure and this more commonly occurs on the back of the dog, near the tail.

**e) Ear Infections**

As a result of their long hanging ears, this dog is commonly prone to ear infection or inflammation, therefore, guardians need to make sure that the ears are kept dry and free of excessive hair growth.

**f) Entropion**

This is a condition in which the dog's eyelid will roll inward which then causes the lashes to rub against the eyeball. Surgery is required to correct this problem.

**g) Cataracts**

Cataracts, which are common in many breeds, is an eye condition where the lens becomes cloudy or milky, which would be like trying to see through a foggy window. This eye condition can appear from birth to 3 years of age and will usually lead to blindness.

**h) Epilepsy**

Epilepsy can display itself with mild to more serious seizures.

**i) Heart Disease**

Heart disease may result from a degeneration of the mitral valve.

If a dog has this problem, the blood will flow back into the chamber, which can cause the chamber to enlarge, which then can cause other problems, including an irregular heartbeat, constricted windpipe, or flowing back into the lungs.

**j) Hypothyroidism**

This is a condition resulting from an inadequate production of thyroid hormone which is treated with medication. Symptoms can include weight gain or obesity, constant hunger, reduced energy and a coarser the feel of the dog's coat texture. Blood samples will be taken in order to test for a malfunctioning thyroid.

**k) Megaesophagus**

This is an enlarged esophagus, and although not life threatening, will require changes in your dog's eating habits. Meals should be given more frequently and in smaller portions while the dog is in the sitting up position, which will take advantage of gravity to help move the food from the dog's oesophagus into the stomach.

**l) Cancer**

Dogs affected by cancer are often those that were not neutered or spayed. Therefore, if you do not require your poodle to remain sexually intact for breeding, it makes sense to have them neutered or spayed.

**m) Damaged Tail**

This is a common injury resulting from the tail being hairless and quite slender, which can cause the tail to split if it is chewed or becomes chapped in cold weather, or if it gets wagged against a hard object.

## 4. American & English Cocker Spaniel

A healthy Cocker Spaniel may or may not be plagued with health problems associated with their breed, and may live an average of 10 to 12 years or longer. Common genetic and other health problems that may afflict a Cocker Spaniel include:

**a) Hip and Elbow Dysplasia**

This is a condition in which the head of the femur fits improperly into the hip or elbow joint socket. Factors that have an influence include nutrition, as this is a dog that suffers from obesity, a dog's environment and the condition of the hips of its parents. Screening for hip dysplasia is recommended for breeding stock.

**b) Luxating Patella**

This slipping kneecap condition is a common defect seen in many breeds, including the Cocker Spaniel, that may also be caused by accidentally falling or jumping from a height. Often you will see a dog with this problem appear to be skipping down the road as they occasionally life one leg when the kneecap slips out of the patellar groove and the leg locks up. Surgery is the treatment option for this condition, although many dogs live a relatively normal life with this defect.

**c) Progressive Retinal Atrophy**

Some Cocker Spaniels can suffer from several eye problems,

including Progressive Retinal Atrophy (PRA). PRA causes degeneration of the retina, which is part of the eye. The retina is the part that senses visual information and sends it to the brain.

Degeneration of this vital part of the eye eventually will lead to blindness. ) This disease usually appears between 3 and 5 years of age. A simple DNA test is available to determine (without waiting for symptoms to appear).

**d) Cataracts**

Cataracts, which are common in many breeds, is an eye condition where the lens becomes cloudy or milky, which would be like trying to see through a foggy window. This eye condition can appear from birth to 3 years of age and will usually lead to blindness.

**e) Glaucoma**

This eye disease, which is usually caused by an increase of fluid pressure in the eye, can cause permanent damage to the dog's vision in the affected eye or eyes, which, if left untreated, can lead to blindness.

**f) Hemolytic Anemia**

This disease is a type of anemia caused by the abnormal breakdown of red blood cells in the blood vessels or other areas of the dog's body. This condition may be mild or life threatening.

**g) Retinal Dysplasia**

This eye disease appears as streaks or dots in the retina of the dog's eye, which can lead to blindness.

**h) Dilated Cardiomyopathy**

This is a disease of the heart that causes that causes weakness in the muscle tissues and a subsequent enlarging of the heart.

**i) Sick Sinus Syndrome**

This is another abnormality of the heart, where the heart beats irregularly causing an arrhythmia of the sinus node of the heart, which is the primary pacemaker of the heart.

A dog suffering from this condition may experience low blood pressure.

**j) Phosphofructokinase Deficiency**

Approximately 10% of the Cocker Spaniel population is affected by this condition, resulting from a recessive gene preventing the proper metabolizing of glucose into energy. A dog with this condition will be very low energy, preventing them from being able to exercise.

DNA testing is possible before breeding in order to prevent two dogs with the same recessive gene from producing puppies with this deficiency.

**k) Epilepsy**

Approximately 10% of the American Cocker Spaniel population can be genetically prone to canine epilepsy, which displays itself with mild to more serious seizures.

**l) Rage Syndrome**

This syndrome is also thought to be an inherited type of epilepsy, which appears as sudden, violent attacks in a dog that is otherwise calm and well behaved.

**m) Ear Infections**

The Cocker Spaniel, because of their long hanging ears are commonly prone to ear infection or inflammation, therefore, guardians need to make sure that the ears are kept dry and free of excessive hair.

As with all purebred canines, many noted health conditions can be prevented when conscientious breeders screen breeding stock.

## 5. Poodle

While a healthy Poodle (depending on their size) may live to be 15 years or more years old, some of the genetic and common health issues may include:

### a) Progressive Retinal Atrophy

Progressive Retinal Atrophy (PRA) can appear at 3-5 years old. A simple DNA test is available to determine (without waiting for symptoms to appear) whether your Miniature Poodle has inherited PRA, or not.

### b) Cataracts

Cataracts can appear from birth to 3 years old and usually lead to blindness. Cataracts appearing after age 3 are usually milder.

### b) Other Eye Problems

Miniature Poodles can also suffer from glaucoma, corneal ulcers, eyelash problems, retinal dysplasia and tear duct disorders.

### c) Otitis Externa

This is an inflammation of the ear canal, which can become chronic, and causes discomfort, irritation and pain. Ear infections are common due to the long narrow ear canals, long ears and profuse hair growth in the ear canals.

### d) Cushing's Disease

There are three forms of Cushing's Disease and most dogs suffer from the more common form, *"Pituitary Dependent PD"*, which is a slow growing form of cancer that is located in the pituitary gland.

**e) Cancer**

Poodles affected by cancer are often those that were not neutered or spayed. Therefore, if you do not require your poodle to remain sexually intact for breeding, it makes sense to have them neutered or spayed.

**f) Hypothyroidism**

This is a condition resulting from an inadequate production of thyroid hormone which is treated with medication. Symptoms can include weight gain or obesity, constant hunger, reduced energy and a coarser the feel of the dog's coat texture. Blood samples will be taken in order to test for a malfunctioning thyroid.

**g) Dental Disease**

Smaller sized Poodles, because of their smaller jaw, are prone to dental disease.

**h) Pancreatitis**

This disease is especially common in middle-aged, overweight Miniature Poodles who are pudgy around the middle because they are over-fed and/or do not get enough daily exercise.

Never suddenly give these dogs a meal or a treat that has a very high fat content, because this is the most common trigger of a pancreatitis attack, which can be fatal.

**i) Epilepsy**

Seizures can occur in all three sizes of Poodle and the most common cause is idiopathic epilepsy, which is an inherited form of epilepsy.

However, many factors can cause seizures and it is very important to have a Miniature Poodle diagnosed if seizures begin.

**j) Heart Disease**

The Miniature Poodle can suffer from degeneration of the mitral valve.

If a dog has this problem, the blood will flow back into the chamber, which can cause the chamber to enlarge, which then can cause other problems, including an irregular heartbeat, constricted windpipe, or flowing back into the lungs.

**k) Hip Dysplasia**

Hip Dysplasia is a condition in which the head of the femur fits improperly into the hip joint socket. Factors that have an influence on the hips include nutrition, a dog's environment and the condition of the hips of its parents. Screening for hip dysplasia is recommended for breeding stock.

**l) Legg-Calve-Perthes Disease**

This is a more serious, but less common disease of the hip joint – degeneration of the head of the femur, which causes severe pain and lameness.

**m) Luxating Patella**

This slipping or floating kneecap condition is a common defect seen in many smaller breeds, including the Miniature Poodle, and may also be caused by accidentally falling or jumping from a height.

Usually the condition will present itself between the ages of 4 and 6 months.

Often you will see a dog with this problem appear to be skipping down the road as they occasionally lift one leg as the kneecap slips out of the patellar groove and the leg locks up.

In more severe cases, surgery may be the recommended treatment option to correct this condition.

**n) Tracheal Collapse**

Collapsing of the trachea creates an airway obstruction of the "*windpipe*," sometimes also referred to as *"reverse sneezing"*.

The trachea is a tube consisting of strong rings of cartilage through which air is transported in and out of the dog's lungs. As air is squeezed through the windpipe during breathing, sometimes the tracheal rings collapse, which causes a coughing or honking sound.

Usually this coughing or honking is brought on by excitement over visiting a new dog or eating an especially tasty treat. As well, sometimes irritants in the environment, such as vehicle exhaust, smoke or dust, may provoke the symptoms.

Further, symptoms can be exacerbated when exercising during hot or humid weather, and more so if the dog is overweight. In mild cases, a honking or coughing session will only last for a few seconds and can be assisted by gently rubbing the dog's nose or giving a quick squeeze around the rib cage to help relax the trachea and get the air flowing again.

In severe cases, surgery is recommended, which involves applying prosthetic rings to the outside of the trachea. The success rate of this tricky operation is reported to be in the 75- to 85% range.

**o) Undescended Testicles**

This condition occurs when a male dog's testicles are trapped in the abdominal cavity, which may sometimes be successfully treated with hormone injections. If the testicles still fail to descend they must be removed in order to prevent increased risk of becoming cancerous.

**p) Von Willebrand Disease**

This is a blood disorder similar to hemophilia in humans where blood does not clot properly, which means that if the dog becomes injured, they are more likely to suffer from excessive bleeding episodes.

There is a simple DNA test available to rule out this disease at any time, rather than waiting for symptoms to appear.

Again, as with all purebred canines, many noted health conditions could be prevented when conscientious breeders screen breeding stock. To ensure that the puppy you may be considering is as healthy as possible, always ask questions about whether the parents of a particular puppy have been screened and are free from the types of health problems that may be inherent in either breed.

Australian Labradoodles are generally quite healthy dogs and, depending on their size, when from healthy breeding stock and well cared for can enjoy an average life expectancy of approximately 10 to 15 years, with some living even longer.

Generally speaking, while the Australian Labradoodle could suffer from any problems inherent in either parent breed, they will usually be much healthier than either of their parents.

## 6. Allergies

One of the most common complaints discussed at the veterinarian's office when they see dogs scratching and chewing at themselves is possible allergies.

Unlike us humans, who react to allergies with nasal symptoms, when our dogs are suffering from allergies they will typically present with itchy skin or ear problems.

### a) Environmental

Allergies are usually first noticed because your Australian Labradoodle is scratching, itching, biting, licking or chewing at their skin or paws.

Just like us humans, our dogs can develop allergies to dust, chemicals, grass, mold, pollen, car exhaust, cigarette smoke, and flea and tick preparations, as well as allergies to materials, such as wool or cotton, and chemicals found in washing soap or chemicals found in cleaning products you use around your home.

Symptoms are usually seen on the stomach, inside of the legs, and at the tail or paws.

Since most allergies are seasonal, our dogs will be more affected in the spring or fall. Airborne irritants inhaled by your Australian Labradoodle, may result in coughing, sneezing or watery eyes.

If you think that your dog may have come in contact with an environmental irritant, the best thing you can do for your dog is give them a cleansing bath, with the proper canine shampoo, followed by canine conditioner.

Remember that an Australian Labradoodle is close to the ground, and the longer their hair, the more they resemble a duster who attracts everything they come into contact with.

### b) Junk Food

*"True"* food allergies usually account for only about 10% of allergy problems in our canine friends.

For instance, itching, chewing and chronic ear infections are not actually caused by food allergies, but rather are the result of a suppressed immune system, which is caused by eating a low quality diet.

These types of food allergies can oftentimes be completely resolved by changing your Australian Labradoodle's diet to a high quality food that is more easily digested.

Proper nutrition is the easiest way to prevent any food allergies.

Many dog food products contain corn, wheat and soybeans, which are common allergens. Usually it is the gluten in these foods that cause the allergic reaction.

Visit your local pet food store and educate yourself or talk with a knowledgeable representative because there's no excuse for feeding your dog a junk food diet when there are so many healthy choices now available that will help your canine companion live a long and healthy life.

## 7. Canine CPR

Of course, nobody wants to ever be put in a situation where the life of their precious canine companion is put at risk, however, the reality is that accidents happen, and therefore, knowing a little bit about how to help save your beloved furry friend is time well spent.

First of all, remember to handle an injured dog very carefully and gently. A dog that is traumatized, fearful or in pain, even one that is usually gentle, may lash out and try to bite.

Consider taking a class, because there are many animal CPR courses being offered these days through community educational systems or even online.

It's also a good idea to have a canine first aid kit both at home and in your vehicle in case of emergencies. Items to include in your first aid kit:

Scissors
Tweezers
Tick Twister
Nail Clippers
Kwik Stop Styptic powder
Gauze bandaging
Non-stick bandages for wounds
Medical tape
Antiseptic wash for wounds, such as hydrogen peroxide
Sterile eyewash
Towel
Washcloth
Blanket

Familiarizing yourself with the American Red Cross emergency techniques outlined in the following chart *("Saving your pet with CPR")* may be exactly what you need to help save the life of your own dog or someone else's.

# Saving your pet with CPR

With pets increasingly being treated like a member of the family, many owners are learning emergency techniques like CPR to keep their pet alive before bringing it to a veterinarian.

**If there is no breathing and no pulse, begin CPR immediately.**

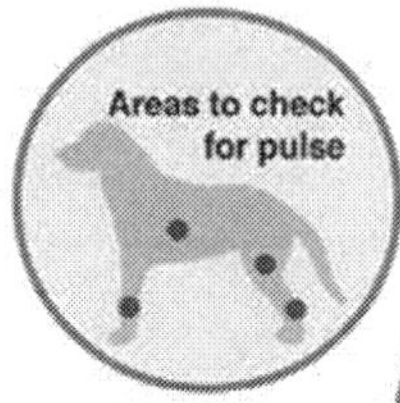


### Check for breathing and pulse

Check pulse using middle and index finger below the wrist, inner thigh (femoral artery), below the ankle or where left elbow touches the chest.

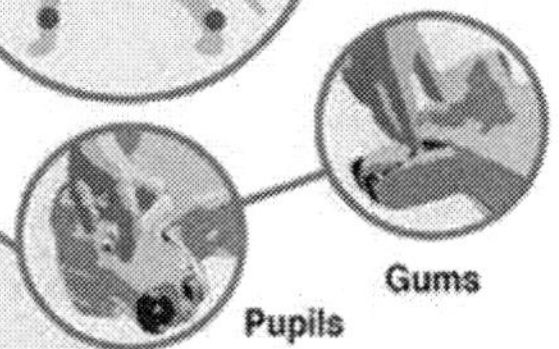


### Look for other warning signs

- Gums and lips will appear gray- colored.
- Pupils will be dilated and not responsive to light.

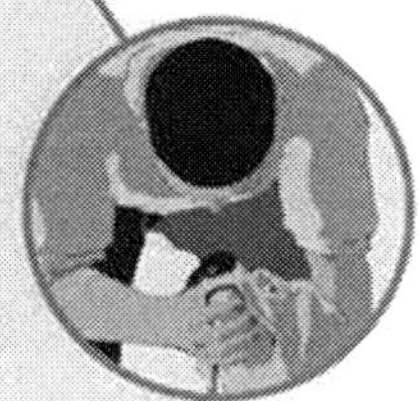

### If not breathing, give breath to animal

**Cats and small dogs**
Place your mouth over its nose and mouth to blow air in.

**Medium–large dogs**
Place your mouth over its nose to blow air in.

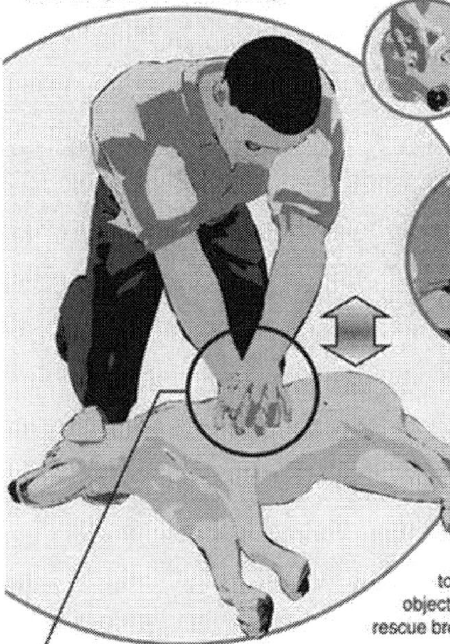

### Heimlich maneuver

If breath won't go in, airway may be blocked. Turn dog upside down, with its back against your chest. Wrap your arms around the dog and clasp your hands together just below its rib cage (since you're holding the dog upside down, it's above the rib cage, in the abdomen). Using both arms, give five sharp thrusts to the abdomen. Then check its mouth or airway for the object. If you see it, remove it and give two more rescue breaths.

### Start compressions if no pulse

Lay animal on right side and place hand over ribs where its elbow touches the chest. Begin compressions. Do not give compressions if dog has pulse.

| Animal size | Compress chest | Compressions per breath of air |
|---|---|---|
| Cat/small dog (Under 30 lbs.) | 1/2-1 inch | 5 |
| Medium–large dog (30–90 lbs.) | 1–3 inches | 5 |
| Giant dog (over 90 lbs.) | 1–3 inches | 10 |

### Repeat procedure

- Check pulse after 1 minute and then every few minutes.
- Continue giving CPR until the animal has a pulse and is breathing.
- Stop CPR after 20 minutes.

SOURCE: American Red Cross

# Chapter 9: Daily Feeding and Care

## 1. Feeding Puppies

For growing puppies, a general feeding rule of thumb is to feed 10% of the puppy's present body weight or between 2% and 3% of their projected adult weight each day.

Keep in mind that high energy puppies will require extra protein to help them grow and develop into healthy adult dogs, especially during their first two years of life.

There are now many foods on the market that are formulated for all stages of a dog's life (including the puppy stage), so whether you choose one of these foods or a food specially formulated for puppies, they will need to be fed smaller meals more frequently throughout the day (3 or 4 times), until they are at least one year of age.

**NOTE**: choose quality sources of meat protein for healthy puppies and dogs, including beef, buffalo, chicken, duck, fish, hare, lamb, ostrich, pork, rabbit, turkey, venison, or any other source of wild meaty protein.

## 2. Feeding Adults

An adult dog will generally need to be fed between 2% and 3% of their body weight each day. Read the labels and avoid foods that contain a high amount of grains and other fillers. Choose foods that list high quality meat protein as the main ingredient.

### Picky Eaters

Be careful that you do not get into the habit of *"doctoring"* your dog's food, which means adding bits and pieces of your human food to make it more tempting for your dog, otherwise, you will inadvertently create a picky eater who will then refuse to eat.

If this has already happened and your dog is refusing to eat his or her dog dinner, so long as you are feeding a high quality (mostly meat) dog food, do not worry, because no dog will starve itself. In fact, if the dog was living in the wild, they often will go 2-3 days without catching any food.

In order to break a dog of the habit of being a picky eater, make sure that you set regular meal times and remove food not eaten approximately 20 minutes after you have presented it to your dog.

It is important that your dog understands that you are in control of their food source, and once they understand this, they will also understand that they have a certain amount of time in which to eat their food.

It is also important to mix your dog's food with your hands, so that your scent is all over the food, before you give it to them to eat. This way you are mimicking what would happen if you were the pack leader our hunting for your food in the wild.

When dogs hunt for their own food, the leader of the pack always gets to eat first while all the other dogs must wait until the leader eats their fill before they can rush in to eat what is left over.

Therefore, when you are mixing your domesticated dog's dinner with your hands, and getting your scent all over the food, you are sending them the subtle message that you are the pack leader and that you are now allowing them to finish the food that was once yours.

**TIP:** grated parmesan cheese sprinkled on a dog's dinner will help to stop picky eaters from ignoring their food while improving their skin and coat. To get the cheese to stick to the kibble, first mix a small amount of olive oil into the kibble, and then sprinkle with finely grated Parmesan cheese.

## 3. Treats

Since the creation of the first dog treat over 150 years ago the myriad of choices available on every pet store, feed store and grocery store shelf almost outnumbers those looking forward to eating them.

Today's treats are not just for making us guilty humans feel better because it makes us happy to give our fur friends something they really enjoy because today's treats are also designed to actually improve our dog's health.

Some of us humans treat our dogs, just because, others use treats for training purposes, others for health, while still others treat for a combination of reasons.

Whatever reason you choose to give treats to your Australian Labradoodle, keep in mind that if we treat our dogs too often throughout the day, we may create a picky eater who will no longer want to eat their regular meals.

As well, if the treats we are giving are high calorie, we may be putting our dog's health in jeopardy by allowing them to become overweight.

**TIP**: an interesting article written by Jonathan O'Callaghan, recently published on June 12, 2014 in the Daily Mail, indicates that researchers in Sweden have discovered that dogs were visibly happier when they had to earn their treats as a reward for completing a task, rather than just being given a treat for looking cute.

Apparently, just like us humans get that happy "eureka" moment when we finally solve a problem, so do our canine counterparts.

If you've been treating your dog for no other reason that just because they looked expectantly at the cookie jar, perhaps now is the time to change your human habits and ask your dog to perform a trick or have to search for a hidden treat, so that your dog can also feel that emotional excitement of being rewarded for accomplishing a task.

## 4. Treats to Avoid

### a) Rawhide

Rawhide is soaked in an ash/lye solution to remove every particle of meat, fat and hair and then further soaked in bleach to remove remaining traces of the ash/lye solution. Now that the product is no longer food, it no longer has to comply with food regulations.

While the hide is still wet it is shaped into rawhide chews, and upon drying it shrinks to approximately 1/4 of its original size.

Further, arsenic based products are often used as preservatives, and antibiotics and insecticides are added to kill bacteria that also fight against good bacteria in your dog's intestines.

The collagen fibers in the rawhide make it very tough and long lasting which makes this chew a popular choice for humans to give to their dogs because it satisfies the dog's natural urge to chew while providing many hours of quiet entertainment.

Sadly, when a dog chews a rawhide treat, they ingest many harsh chemicals and when your dog swallows a piece of rawhide, that piece now can swell up to four times its size inside your dog's stomach, which can cause anything from mild to severe gastric blockages that could become life threatening and require surgery.

### b) Pig Ears

These treats are actually the ears of pigs, and while most dogs will eagerly devour them, they are extremely high in fat, which can cause stomach upsets, vomiting and diarrhea for many dogs.

Pig ears are often processed and preserved with unhealthy chemicals that discerning dog guardians will not want to feed their dogs.

As well, the ears are often quite thin and crispy and when the dog chews them pieces can break off, like chips, and can easily become stuck in a dog's throat.

While pig ears are generally not considered to be a healthy treat choice for any dog, they should be especially avoided for any dog that may be at risk of being overweight.

### c) Hoof Treats

Many humans give cow, horse and pig hooves to their dogs as treats because they consider them to be *"natural"*.

The truth is that after processing these *"treats"* they retain little, if any, of their *"natural"* qualities.

Hoof treats are processed with harsh preservatives, including insecticides, lead, bleach, arsenic based products, and antibiotics to kill bacteria, that can also harm the good bacteria in your dog's intestines, and if all bacteria is not killed in these meat based products before feeding them to your dog, they could also suffer from Salmonella poisoning.

Hooves can also cause chipping or breaking of your dog's teeth as well as perforation or blockages in your dog's intestines.

## 5. Healthy Treats

### a) Hard Treats

There are so many choices of hard, or crunchy treats available that come in many varieties of shapes, sizes and flavors, that you may have a difficult time choosing.

If your Australian Labradoodle will eat them, hard treats will help to keep their teeth cleaner.

Whatever you do choose, be certain to read the labels and make sure that the ingredients are high quality and appropriately sized for your Australian Labradoodle friend.

**b) Soft Treats**

Soft, chewy treats are also available in endless varieties and flavors, suitable for all the different needs of our fur friends and are often used for training purposes as they have a stronger smell.

**c) Dental Treats**

Dental treats or chews are designed with the specific purpose of helping your Australian Labradoodle to maintain healthy teeth and gums.

They usually require intensive chewing and are often shaped with high ridges and bumps to exercise the jaw and massage gums while removing plaque build-up near the gum line.

**d) Freeze-Dried and Jerky Treats**

Freeze-dried and jerky treats offer a tasty morsel most dogs find irresistible as they are usually made of simple, meaty ingredients, such as liver, poultry and seafood.

These treats are usually lightweight and easy to carry around, which means they can also be great as training treats.

**e) Human Food Treats**

You will want to be very careful when feeding human foods to dogs as treats, because many of our foods contain additives and ingredients that could be toxic and harmful.

Be certain to choose simple, fresh foods with minimal or no processing, such as lean meat, poultry or seafood, and even if your Australian Labradoodle will eat anything put in front of them, be aware that many common human foods, such as grapes, raisins, onions and chocolate are poisonous to dogs.

### f) Training Treats

While any sort of treat can be used as an extra incentive during training sessions, soft treats are often used for training purposes because of their stronger smell and smaller sizes.

Yes, we humans love to treat our dogs, whether for helping to teach the new puppy to go pee outside, teaching the adolescent dog new commands, for trick training, for general good behavior, or for no reason at all, other than that they just gave us the *"look"*.

Generally, the treats you feed your dog should not make up more than approximately 10% of their daily food intake, so make sure the treats you choose are high quality, so that you can help to keep your Australian Labradoodle both happy and healthy.

## 6. Choosing the Right Food

In order to choose the right food for your Australian Labradoodle, first, it's important to understand a little bit about canine physiology and what Mother Nature intended when she created our fur friends.

More than 230 years ago, in 1785, the English Sportman's dictionary described the best diet for a dog's health in an article entitled *"Dog"*.

This article indicated that the best food for a dog was something called "Greaves", described as "the sediment of melted tallow. It is made into cakes for dogs' food. In Scotland and parts of the US it is called cracklings."

Out of the meager beginning of the first commercially made dog food has sprung a massively lucrative and vastly confusing industry that has only recently begun to evolve beyond those early days of feeding our dogs the dregs of human leftovers because it was cheap and convenient for us humans.

Even today, the majority of dog food choices have far more to do with being convenient for humans to store and serve than it does with being a diet truly designed to be a nutritionally balanced, healthy food choice for a canine.

The dog food industry is big business and as such, because there are now almost limitless choices, there is much confusion and endless debate when it comes to answering the question, *"What is the best food for my dog?"*

Educating yourself, by talking to experts and reading everything you can find on the subject, plus taking into consideration several relevant factors, will help to answer the dog food question for you and your dog.

For instance, where you live may dictate what sorts of foods you have access to. Other factors to consider will include the particular requirements of your dog, such as their age, energy and activity levels.

Next will be expense, time and quality. While we all want to give our dogs the best food possible, many humans lead very busy lives and cannot, for instance, prepare their own dog food, but still want to feed a high quality diet that fits within their budget.

However, perhaps most important when choosing an appropriate diet for our dogs, is learning to be more observant of Mother Nature's design and taking a closer look at our dog's teeth, jaws and digestive tract.

While humans are herbivores who derive energy from eating plants, our canine companions are carnivores, which means that they derive their energy and nutrient requirements from eating a diet consisting mainly or exclusively of the flesh of animal tissues (in other words, meat).

**a) The Canine Teeth**

The first part of your dog you will want to take a good look at when considering what to feed will be their teeth.

Unlike humans, who are equipped with wide, flat molars for grinding grains, vegetables and other plant-based materials, canine teeth are all pointed because they are designed to rip, shred and tear into animal meat and bone.

**b) The Canine Jaw**

Another obvious consideration when choosing an appropriate food source for our fur friends, is the fact that every canine is born equipped with powerful jaws and neck muscles for the specific purpose of being able to pull down and tear apart their hunted prey.
The structure of the jaw of every canine is such that it opens widely to hold large pieces of meat and bone, while the actual mechanics of a dog's jaw permits only vertical (up and down) movement that is designed for crushing.

**c) The Canine Digestive Tract**

A dog's digestive tract is short and simple and designed to move their natural choice of food (hide, meat and bone) quickly through their systems.

Vegetables and plant matter require more time to break down in the gastrointestinal tract, which in turn, requires a more complex digestive system than the canine body is equipped with.

The canine digestive system is simply unable to break down vegetable matter, which is why whole vegetables look pretty much the same going into your dog as they do coming out the other end.

Given the choice, most dogs would never choose to eat plants or vegetables and fruits over meat, however, we humans continue to feed them a kibble based diet that contains high amounts of vegetables, fruits and grains and low amounts of meat.

Plus, in order to get our dogs to eat fruits, vegetables and grains we usually have to flavor the food with meat or meat by-products.

How much healthier and long lived might our beloved fur friends be if, instead of largely ignoring nature's design for our canine companions, we chose to feed them whole, unprocessed, species-appropriate food?

With many hundreds of dog food brands to choose from, it's no wonder we humans are confused about what to feed our dogs to help them live long and healthy lives.

Following are some suggestions and questions that may help you choose a dog food company that you can feel comfortable with:

- How long have they have been in business?
- Is dog food their main industry?
- Are they dedicated to their brand?
- Are they easily accessible?
- Do they honestly answer your questions?
- Do they have a good Company Safety Standard?
- Do they set higher standards?
- Read the ingredients - where did they come from?
- Are the ingredients something you would eat?
- Are the ingredients farmed locally?
- Was it cooked using standards you would trust?
- Is the company certified under human food or organic guidelines?

Whatever you decide to feed your Australian Labradoodle, keep in mind that, just as too much wheat, other grains and other fillers in our human diet is having detrimental effects on our human health, the same can be very true for our best fur friends.

Our dogs are also suffering from many of the same life threatening diseases that are commonly found in our human society (heart disease, cancer, diabetes, obesity), which all have a direct correlation to eating genetically altered foods that are no longer pure, in favor of a convenient, processed and packaged diet.

## 7. The Raw Diet

While more and more of us humans are coming to the belief that we are killing ourselves and our dogs with processed foods, others believe that there are dangers involved in feeding raw foods to our fur friends.

Those who are raw feeding advocates believe that the ideal diet for their dog is one which would be very similar to what a dog living in the wild would have access to hunting or foraging, and these canine guardians are often opposed to feeding their dog any sort of commercially manufactured pet foods, because they consider them to be poor substitutes.

On the other hand, those opposed to feeding their dogs a raw or biologically appropriate raw food diet, believe that the risks associated with food-borne illnesses during the handling and feeding of raw meats outweigh the purported benefits.

Interestingly, even though the United States Food and Drug Administration (FDA) states that they do not advocate a raw diet for dogs, they do advise for those who wish to take this route, that following basic hygiene guidelines for handling raw meat can minimize any associated risks.

Further, high pressure pasteurization (HPP), which is high pressure, water based technology for killing bacteria, is USDA-approved for use on organic and natural food products, and is being utilized by many commercial raw pet food manufacturers.

Interestingly, raw meats purchased at your local grocery store contain a much higher level of acceptable bacteria than raw food produced for dogs because the meat purchased for human consumption is supposed to be cooked, which will kill any bacteria that might be present.

This means that canine guardians feeding their dogs a raw food diet can be quite certain that commercially prepared raw foods sold in pet stores will be safer than raw meats purchased in grocery stores.

Many guardians of high energy, working breed dogs will agree that their dogs thrive on a raw or BARF (Biologically Appropriate Raw Food) diet and strongly believe that the potential benefits of feeding a raw dog food diet are many, including:

- Healthy, shiny coats
- Decreased shedding
- Fewer allergy problems
- Healthier skin
- Cleaner teeth
- Fresher breath
- Increased energy levels
- Improved digestion
- Smaller stools
- Strengthened immune system
- Increased mobility in arthritic pets
- Increase or improvement in overall health

All dogs, of every size, whether working breed or companion dogs are amazing athletes in their own right, therefore every dog deserves to be fed the best food available.

A raw diet is a direct evolution of what dogs ate before they became our domesticated pets and we turned toward commercially prepared, easy to serve dry dog food that required no special storage or preparation.

The BARF diet is all about feeding our dogs what they are designed to eat by returning them to their wild, evolutionary diet.

## 8. The Dehydrated Diet

Dehydrated dog food comes in both raw meat and cooked meat forms and these foods are usually air dried to reduce moisture to the level where bacterial growth is inhibited.

The appearance of de-hydrated dog food is very similar to dry kibble and the typical feeding methods include adding warm water before serving, which makes this type of diet both healthy for our dogs and convenient for us to serve.

Dehydrated recipes are made from minimally processed fresh whole foods to create a healthy and nutritionally balanced meal that will meet or exceed the dietary requirements of a healthy canine.

Dehydrating removes only the moisture from the fresh ingredients, which usually means that because the food has not already been cooked at a high temperature, more of the overall nutrition is retained.

A de-hydrated diet is a convenient way to feed your dog a nutritious diet because all you have to do is add warm water, and wait five minutes while the food re-hydrates so your Australian Labradoodle can enjoy a warm meal.

## 9. The Kibble Diet

While many canine guardians are starting to take a closer look at the food choices they are making for their furry companions, there is no mistaking that the convenience and relative economy of dry dog food kibble, that had its beginnings in the 1940's, continues to be the most popular pet food choice for most dog friendly humans.

Some 75 years later, the massive pet food industry offers up a confusingly large number of choices with hundreds of different manufacturers and brand names lining the shelves of veterinarian offices, grocery stores and pet food aisles.

While feeding a high quality bagged kibble diet that has been flavored to appeal to dogs and supplemented with vegetables and fruits to appeal to humans, may keep most Australian Labradoodle companions happy and relatively healthy, you will ultimately need to decide whether this is the best diet for them.

## 10. The Right Bowl

Following is a brief description of the different categories and types of dog bowls that would be appropriate choices for your Australian Labradoodle's particular needs.

**Automatic Watering Bowls**: are standard dog bowls (often made out of plastic) that are attached to a reservoir container, which is designed to keep water constantly available to your dog as long as there is water remaining in the storage compartment.

**Ceramic/Stoneware Bowls**: an excellent choice for those who like options in personality, color and shape.

**Elevated Bowls**: raised dining table dog bowls are a tidy and classy choice that will make your dog's dinner time a more comfortable experience while getting the bowls off the floor.

**No Skid Bowls**: are for dogs that push their bowls across the floor when eating. A non-skid dog bowl will help keep the feed bowl where you put it.

**No Tip Bowls**: are designed to prevent the messy type of doggy eater from flipping over their dinner or water bowls.

**Slow Feeder Bowls**: Many of our canine companions eat their food so quickly that it can literally cause health issues, such as choking, digestion problems, throwing up, and bloat that can cause death from gulping too much air with their food.

These specialty bowls are known by several different names, including *"Anti-Gulp", "Go Slow", "Slow Feeder",* and *"Slow Me Down"*, and if your dog is wolfing their food, this will be the best type of feed bowl to slow down the dog that hoovers down their dinner in record time.

**TIP**: if you don't want to spend the money on a specialty slow feeder bowl, find yourself a fist-sized, smooth round rock and place it in the middle of your dog's stainless bowl so they have to work their way around the rock to get to their food. This will do the job of slowing them down just as effectively.

**Stainless Steel Bowls**: are as close to indestructible as a bowl can be, plus they are sanitary, easy to clean and water stays cooler for a longer period of time in a stainless bowl.

**Wooden Bowls**: for those humans concerned about stylish home decor, wooden dog bowl dining stations are beautiful pieces of furniture unto themselves that can enhance your home decor.

**Travel Bowls**: are a convenient, practical and handy addition for every canine travel kit.

Consider a space saving, collapsible dog bowl, made out of hygienic, renewable bamboo that comes in fun colors and different sizes, making it perfect for every travel bowl needs.

If you would like to learn more about all the many dog bowl choices available, visit DogBowlForYourDog.com, which is a comprehensive, one-stop website dedicated to explaining the ins and outs of every food bowl imaginable and helping you find the perfect bowl for all your Australian Labradoodle's needs.

## 11. Exercise

All of our canine companions are amazing, natural athletes and because of this, they need daily exercise to stay fit, happy and healthy.

The highly energetic Australian Labradoodle is no exception to this rule. Every Australian Labradoodle plenty of daily exercise, and will love going for walks or running with you or engaging in any manner of canine sport with their guardian several times every day.

As well, taking your Australian Labradoodle for a disciplined walk, where they are on leash and calmly walking beside you without straining on the leash or trying to lead you, will reinforce that you are the boss and they are the follower.

Any type of disciplined exercise you can engage in with your Australian Labradoodle will help to exercise both their body and their intelligent mind and will burn off pent up daily energy reserves so that your Australian Labradoodle will be a happy and contented companion.

If you find that your Australian Labradoodle is being a pest by chewing inappropriate items around the home or being demanding of your time, or especially unruly when visitors come to call, this is likely because they are not being challenged enough or exercised often enough, or long enough each day to drain out their daily pent up energy reserves.

A healthy, adult Australian Labradoodle will thrive when being walked several times each day and will enjoy the challenge of being engaged in other forms of disciplined activity, such as Obedience, Rally, Flyball, Frisbee, Trick Training, Freestyle Dance, or Agility.

## 12. Playtime

Every dog needs some regular playtime each day, and this is even more important with an active breed, such as the Australian Labradoodle, who will be your loving, playful, energetic companion.

While every Australian Labradoodle will be different with respect to what types of games they may enjoy, most Australian Labradoodle's will really love any game involving retrieving and it would be the rare Australian Labradoodle that did not live for the opportunity to swim and retrieve a stick or float.

A fun game of *"Search"*, where you ask your Australian Labradoodle to "Sit/Stay" while you hide a favorite treat that they then have to use their nose to find, will appeal to almost every dog.

After a disciplined walk with your Australian Labradoodle, they will also enjoy being given the opportunity for some off leash freedom to really stretch out by running free to play and socialize with other similar sized dogs.

## 13. Daily Grooming

Daily grooming is a must for any healthy Australian Labradoodle.

Get into the routine of spending at least 15 minutes each day brushing or combing your Australian Labradoodle, checking their ears and nails and brushing their teeth.

## 14. Safe Traveling

Far too many canine guardians do nothing to protect their companions when traveling with them inside their vehicles.

According to a 2011 American Automobile Association study, only about 16% of dog owners restrain their pets when riding in a vehicle, and of those who are trying, many are not properly securing their beloved pets.

That leaves 84% of people who let their dogs roam freely about the inside of their vehicles, leaving them at serious risk of being injured or killed in an automobile accident.

For example, when a vehicle traveling at only 30 miles per hour (48.28 kilometers per hour) is involved in an accident, a small, ten pound (4.54 kg), unrestrained dog will be subjected to approximately 300 pounds force (136 kilogram-force), which is certainly enough to seriously injure or kill an Australian Labradoodle.

There is no denying that dogs that are not properly restrained become projectiles in any sort of vehicle crash.

As well, many drivers permit their smaller dogs to sit on their lap when driving, which is not only distracting to the driver, but if involved in an accident, the vehicle's airbags will deploy at 300 mph (482.8 kilometers per hour) which can easily snap the neck of a small dog.

**a) Faulty Restraints**

Many dog lovers may be laboring under the misconception that they are doing the right thing by buckling their canine companions into a safety harness because they are unaware that many of these dog harnesses that are supposed to keep furry passengers safe have a 100% failure rate.

Statistics collected by the Center for Pet Safety (CPS) have shown that every popular restraint tested with dog dummies, traveling at a sedate 30 mph (48.28 km/h), not only failed, but also indicated that serious injuries or deaths were highly likely.

Most restraints that were tested in the CPS study allowed dogs to easily become flying projectiles during vehicle accidents because the harnesses were simply not strong enough to keep them in their seats, and in many cases the restraints could actually choke the dog during a crash.

When the MGA Research Corporation carried out a pilot study for The Center for Pet Safety (CPS), in which they tested 12 major brands of pet harnesses, the results indicated a 100% failure rate.

According to the American Kennel Club, these safety harness tests were carried out using the average weights of the ten most popular breeds of dogs, including the Labrador Retriever, the German Shepherd, the Golden Retriever, the Beagle, the Bulldog, the Labrador Retriever, the Boxer, the Poodle, the Rottweiler and the Poodle.

The founder and chairman of CPS, believes that, "Saying that these products prevent your pet from becoming a projectile in an accident is a potentially misleading statement."

Law enforcement agencies, safety advocates, insurance companies, and concerned dog owners need to keep pressing for the development of a standard for dog safety equipment, to insist that all such equipment pass a government regulated crash test before being sold as safe for travel.

The safest travel arrangement for any dog is to secure them inside a kennel, followed by finding a safety restraint that is crash and strength tested and certified to be safe for your dog.

**b) Kennels**

If you opt to contain your best friend inside a kennel or crate, you absolutely must make sure that the kennel or bag is very securely attached with the vehicle's seatbelt system or even better, with special tie downs that are bolted to the floor of the vehicle.

A dog kennel or crate will easily fit on the back seat of most vehicles and can be secured with the vehicle's restraint system. An Australian Labradoodle riding inside a kennel inside your vehicle will have the best protection in the case of a rollover accident.

**c) Harness Restraints**

The Kurgo Tru-Fit Smart harness has been crash and strength tested and with its steel nesting buckles has a tensile strength tested to withstand a force of 2250 pounds (1020 kilogram-force). The crash test videos of this product depict a 35-pound (15.9 kilogram) dummy dog traveling at 30 miles per hour (48.28 km/h), recorded at an accredited University test facility.

The Ruff Rider Roadie® harness successfully passed the preliminary test criteria for both dynamic and static load limits. Ruff Rider's only product is the Roadie® travel restraint which was invented by dog owner, Carl Goldberg, after his pet was ejected through the front windshield of his vehicle during a minor collision.

The design of the Roadie® is so unique that it was awarded three (3) patents, and over the past 20 years Roadie® has helped protect many dogs during vehicle accidents.

Sleepypod™ manufactures a safety harness called *"Clickit Utility"* that has a #1 safety rating. Apparently, this harness is the first dog safety harness to incorporate three-points of attachment to better absorb force caused in a front end collision by effectively dissipating energy while keeping the dog in the car seat during an impact (patents pending).

The Clickit Utility harness can also be used in the cargo area and includes a d-ring on the back of the vest so it can be used as a walking harness.

Keep your Australian Labradoodle safe when traveling in your vehicle. Do your research and either transport your dog inside a kennel, or find a safety harness that is both strength tested and certified to be able to keep your Australian Labradoodle safe in the event of an accident.

**d) Sherpa for Small Dogs**

*"Sherpa"* is a name that refers to a soft-sided dog carrier with zippered pockets for carrying important papers, treats, bags, etc., that has mesh sides for superior ventilation.

While there is an actual "Sherpa" brand name, this name has become synonymous with any type of soft-sided carrier bag.

The Sherpa bag has handles as well as a shoulder strap and some even have wheels, so your smaller Australian Labradoodle puppy will be able to safely travel anywhere in style and comfort.

The puppy or smaller sized Australian Labradoodle will be the perfect candidate for learning to travel about inside a Sherpa or soft-sided travel bag, such as the Sleepypod™.

When they are young puppies, get them used to Sherpa travel by putting them inside their bag every time they need to go outside, and before you bring them back inside. When you do this, an Australian Labradoodle puppy will very quickly learn to love scooting into their bag because they associate it with the fun activity of going outside with you.

Once your Australian Labradoodle puppy becomes used to Sherpa travel, it will be very easy for them to travel with you wherever you go, including public transportation (buses), boats, planes and vehicles, and the best way to start them getting used to this idea is as soon as you bring your new puppy home.

Every time you go to your vehicle, put your Australian Labradoodle inside their Sherpa bag and pretty soon they will associate fun adventures with the Sherpa and will not hesitate to quickly hop inside.

*"Sleepypod™"* manufactures various styles of higher end travel bags for smaller dogs, and puts their bags through rigorous crash testing to ensure they are totally safe.

Although these bags are considerably more costly than many other canine travel bags, you will have peace of mind knowing that your Australian Labradoodle will always be safe when riding inside one.

**e) Air Travel**

While most Australian Labradoodles will be too large to travel inside a Sherpa bag inside the airplane cabin, a smaller Australian Labradoodle or a puppy, can be *"carry on baggage"* if the carrier conforms to the airline regulations, which state that a pet carrier must be able to fit under the seat in front of you.

Most soft carriers are airline approved and under seat dimensions are generally as follows:

Window Seat: 19" L x 14" W x 8.25" H
[48.26 cm L x 35.56 cm W x 20.955 cm H]
Middle Seat: 19" L x 19" W x 8.25" H
[48.26 cm L x 48.26 cm W x 20.955 cm H]
Aisle Seat: 19" L x 14" W x 8.25" H
[48.26 cm L x 35.56 cm W x 20.955 cm H]

For in-cabin travel by plane, your dog must be able to stand up and turn around comfortably inside the bag. Airlines also require an absorbent liner in the bag, which could be a pee pad, an old towel, a favorite blanket, or a cozy, faux lambskin liner.

Many styles of canine carrier bags are officially approved for airline travel, and when you make your flight reservations, don't forget to reserve for your Australian Labradoodle as well because there is generally a small charge for in-cabin travel and some airlines will only permit a certain number of canine travelers per flight.

Australian Labradoodles that are too large to fit inside a Sherpa bag will need to be transported inside a hard-sided kennel inside the airplane cargo hold.

# Chapter 10: House Training

## 1. Human Training

House training, house breaking, or *"potty"* training, is a critical first step in the education of any new puppy, and the first part of a successful process is training the human guardian.

When you bring home your new Australian Labradoodle puppy, they will be relying upon your guidance to teach them what they need to learn.

When you provide your puppy with your consistent patience and understanding, they are capable of learning rules at a very early age, and house training is no different, especially since it's all about establishing a regular routine.

Potty training a new puppy takes time and patience — how much time depends entirely upon you.

Check in with yourself and make sure your energy remains consistently calm and patient and that you exercise plenty of compassion and understanding while you help your new puppy learn their new bathroom rules.

Australian Labradoodle puppies and dogs flourish with routines and happily, so do humans, therefore, the first step is to establish a daily routine that will work well for both canine and human alike.

For instance, depending upon the age of your Australian Labradoodle puppy, make a plan to take them out for a bathroom break every two hours and stick to it because while you are in the beginning stages of potty training, the more vigilant and consistent you can be, the quicker and more successful your results will be.

Generally speaking, while your puppy is still growing, a young puppy can hold it approximately one hour for every month of their age.

This means that if your 2-month-old puppy has been happily snoozing for a couple of hours, as soon as they wake up, they will need to go outside.

Some of the first indications or signs that your puppy needs to be taken outside to relieve themselves will be when you see them:

- Sniffing around
- Circling
- Looking for or approaching the door
- Whining, crying or barking
- Acting agitated

It will be important to always take your Australian Labradoodle puppy out first thing every morning, and immediately after they wake up from a nap as well as soon after they have finished eating a meal or having a big drink of water.

Also, your happy praise goes a long way toward encouraging and reinforcing future success when your Australian Labradoodle puppy makes the right decisions, so let them know you are happy when they do their business in the right place.

Initially, treats can be a good way to reinforce how pleased you are that your puppy is learning to go potty in the right place. Slowly treats can be removed and replaced with your happy praise.

Next, now that you have a new puppy in your life, you will want to be flexible with respect to adapting your schedule to meet the requirements that will help to quickly teach your Australian Labradoodle puppy their new bathroom routine.

This means not leaving your puppy alone for endless hours at a time because firstly, they are sensitive pack animals that need companionship and your direction at all times, plus long periods alone will result in the disruption of the potty training schedule you have worked hard to establish.

If you have no choice but to leave your puppy alone for many hours, make sure that you place them in a paper lined room or pen where they can relieve themselves without destroying your favorite carpet or new hardwood flooring.

Remember, your Australian Labradoodle is a growing puppy with a bladder and bowels that they do not yet have complete control over and you will have a much happier time and better success if you simply train yourself to pay attention to when your young companion is showing signs of needing to relieve themselves.

## 2. Bell Training

A very easy way to introduce your new Australian Labradoodle puppy to house training is to begin by teaching them how to ring a doorbell whenever they need to go outside.

Ringing a doorbell is not only a convenient alert system for both you and your Australian Labradoodle puppy or dog, your visitors will be most impressed by how smart your Australian Labradoodle is.

A further benefit of training your puppy to ring a bell is that you will not have to listen to your puppy or dog whining, barking or howling to be let out, and your door will not become scratched up from their nails.

Unless you prefer to purchase an already manufactured doggy doorbell or system, take a trip to your local novelty store and purchase a small bell that has a nice, loud ring.

Attach the bell to a piece of ribbon or string and hang it from a door handle or tape it to a door sill near the door where you will be taking your puppy out when they need to relieve themselves. The string will need to be long enough so that your Australian Labradoodle puppy can easily reach the bell with their nose or a paw.

Next, each time you take your puppy out to go potty, say the word *"Out"*, and use their paw or their nose to ring the bell. Praise them for this *"trick"* and immediately take them outside.

The only down side to teaching your Australian Labradoodle puppy or dog to ring a bell when they want to go outside, is that even if they don't actually have to go out to relieve themselves, but just want to go outside because they are bored, you will still have to take them out every time they ring the bell.

There are many types and styles of *"gotta' go"* commercially manufactured bells you could choose, ranging from the elegant **"Poochie Bells™"** that hang from a doorknob, the simple **"Tell Bell™"** that sits on the floor, or various high tech door chime systems that function much like a doggy intercom system where they push a pad with their paw and it rings a bell.

Whatever doorbell system you choose for your Australian Labradoodle puppy, once they are trained, this type of an alert system is an easy way to eliminate accidents in the home.

## 3. Kennel Training

Kennel training is always a good idea for any puppy early in their education, because it can be utilized for many different situations, including keeping them safe while traveling inside a vehicle and being a very helpful tool for house training.

When purchasing a kennel for your Australian Labradoodle puppy, always buy a kennel that will be the correct size for your puppy once they become an adult.

The kennel will be the correct size if an adult Australian Labradoodle can stand up and easily turn around inside their kennel.

When you train your Australian Labradoodle puppy to accept sleeping in their own kennel at nighttime, this will also help to accelerate their potty training, because no puppy or dog wants to relieve themselves where they sleep, which means that they will hold their bladder and bowels as long as they possibly can.

Always be kind and compassionate and remember that a puppy will be able to hold it approximately one hour for every month of their age.

Generally, an Australian Labradoodle puppy that is three months old will be able to hold it for approximately three hours, unless they just ate a meal or had a big drink of water.

Be watchful and consistent so that you learn your Australian Labradoodle puppy's body language, which will alert you to when it's time for them to go outside.

Presenting them with familiar scents, by taking them to the same spot in the yard or the same street corner, will help to remind and encourage them that they are outside to relieve themselves.

Use a voice cue to remind your puppy why they are outside, such as *"go pee"* and always remember to praise them every time they relieve themselves in the right place so that they quickly understand what you expect of them and will learn to *"go"* on cue.

## 4. Exercise Pen Training

The exercise pen is a transition from kennel only training and will be helpful for those times when you may have to leave your Australian Labradoodle puppy for more hours than they can reasonably be expected to hold it.

During those times when you must be away from the home for several hours, it's time to introduce your Australian Labradoodle puppy to an exercise pen.

Exercise pens are usually constructed of wire sections that you can put together in whatever shape you desire, and the pen needs to be large enough to hold your puppy's kennel inside one half of the pen, while the other half will be lined with newspapers or pee pads.

Place your Australian Labradoodle puppy's food and water dishes next to the kennel and leave the kennel door open, so they can wander in and out whenever they wish, to eat or drink or go to the papers or pads if they need to relieve themselves.

Your puppy will be contained in a small area of your home while you are away and because they are already used to sleeping inside their kennel, they will not want to relieve themselves inside the area where they sleep. Therefore, your Australian Labradoodle puppy will naturally go to the other half of the pen to relieve themselves on the newspapers or pee pads.

This method will help train your puppy to be quickly "paper" trained when you must leave them alone for a few hours.

## 5. Puppy Apartment™ Training

A similar and more costly alternative, the *Puppy Apartment*™ is a step up from the exercise pen training system that makes the process of crate or pen training even easier on both humans and puppies.

The Puppy Apartment™ works well in a variety of situations, whether you're at home and unable to pay close attention to your Australian Labradoodle puppy's needs, whether you must be away from the home for a few hours or during the evening when everyone is asleep and you don't particularly want to get up at

3:00 a.m. to take your Australian Labradoodle puppy out to go pee.

The Puppy Apartment™ is an innovation that is convenient for both puppy and human alike.

What makes this system so effective is the patent pending dividing wall with a door leading to the other side, all inside the pen.

One side of the Puppy Apartment™ is where the puppy's bed is located and the other side (through the doorway) is the bathroom area that is lined with pee pads.

With the bathroom right next door, your Australian Labradoodle puppy or dog can take a bathroom break whenever they wish, without the need to alert family members to let them out.

This one bedroom, one bathroom system, which is a combination of the kennel/training pen, is a great alternative for helping to eliminate the stress of worrying about always keeping a watchful eye on your puppy or getting up during the night to take them outside every few hours to help them avoid making mistakes.

According to Modern Puppies...

> *"The Puppy Apartment™ takes the MESSY out of paper training, the ODORS AND HASSLES out of artificial grass training, MISSING THE MARK out of potty pad training and HAVING TO HOLD IT out of crate training. House training a puppy has never been faster or easier!*
>
> *The Puppy Apartment™ has taken all the benefits of the most popular potty training methods and combined them into one magical device and potty training system. This device and system has revolutionized how modern puppies are potty trained!"*

Manufactured in the United States, this product ships directly from the California supplier (Modern Puppies).

Pricing of the Puppy Apartment™ begins at $138. USD (£83.37) and is only available online at Modern Puppies.

## 6. Free Training

If you would rather not confine your young Australian Labradoodle puppy to one or two rooms in your home, and will be allowing them to freely range about your home anywhere they wish during the day, this is considered free training.

When free house training your Australian Labradoodle puppy, you will need to closely watch your puppy's activities all day long so that you can be aware of the *"signs"* that will indicate when they need to go outside to relieve themselves.

For instance, circling and sniffing is a sure sign that they are looking for a place to do their business.

Never get upset or scold a puppy for having an accident inside the home, because this will result in teaching your puppy to be afraid of you and to only relieve themselves in secret places or when you're not watching.

If you catch your Australian Labradoodle puppy making a mistake, all that is necessary is for you to calmly say *"No"*, and quickly scoop them up and take them outside or to their indoor bathroom area.

From your sensitive puppy's point of view, yelling or screaming when they make a potty mistake, will be understood by your puppy or dog as unstable energy being displayed by the person who is supposed to be their leader. This type of unstable behavior will only teach your puppy to fear and disrespect you.

When you are vigilant, the Australian Labradoodle should not a difficult puppy to housebreak and they will generally do very well when you start them off with *"puppy pee pads"* that you will move closer and closer to the same door that you always use when taking them outside. This way they will quickly learn to associate going to this door when they need to relieve themselves.

When you pay close attention to your Australian Labradoodle puppy's sleeping, eating, drinking and playing habits, you will quickly learn their body language so that you are able to predict when they might need to relieve themselves.

Your Australian Labradoodle puppy will always need to relieve themselves first thing in the morning, as soon as they wake up from a nap, approximately 20 minutes after they finish eating a meal, after they have finished a play session, and of course, before they go to bed at night.

It's important to have compassion during this house training time in your young Australian Labradoodle's life so that their education will be as stress-free as possible.

It's also important to be vigilant because how well you pay attention will minimize the opportunities your puppy may have for making a bathroom mistake in the first place, and the fewer mistakes they make, the sooner your Australian Labradoodle puppy will be house trained.

## 7. Mistakes Happen

Remember that a dog's sense of smell is at least 2,000 times more sensitive that our human sense of smell.

As a result of your Australian Labradoodle puppy's superior sense of smell, it will be very important to effectively remove all odors from house training accidents, because otherwise, your Australian Labradoodle puppy will be attracted by the smell to the place where they may have had a previous accident, and will want to do their business there again and again.

While there are many products that are supposed to remove odors and stains, many of these are not very effective. You want a professional grade cleaner that will not just mask one odor with another scent, you want a product that will completely neutralize odors.

**TIP**: go to RemoveUrineOdors.com and order yourself some *"SUN"* and/or *"Max Enzyme"* because these products contain professional-strength odor neutralizers and urine digesters that bind to and completely absorb odors on any type of surface.

## 8. Electronic Training Devices

Generally speaking, positive training methods are far more effective than using devices that involve negative stimulation.

Further, unless you are training a Australian Labradoodle to hunt badgers or rabbits, using electronic devices is usually a excuse for a lazy human who will not take the time to properly train their dog by teaching them rules and boundaries which leads to respect and an attentive follower.

When you do not provide your Australian Labradoodle (or any dog) with a consistent leadership role that teaches your dog to trust, respect and listen to you in all circumstances, you will inevitably experience behavioral issues.

Electronic training devices such as e-collars, spray collars or electronic fencing all rely upon negative, painful or stressful reinforcement, which can easily cause a sensitive breed, like the Australian Labradoodle, to become nervous or live a life of fear.

For instance, a dog simply cannot understand the principles of "invisible" boundaries, and therefore, should never be subjected to the confusion of the punishment that occurs when walking across an invisible line within their own home territory.

Dogs naturally understand the positive training methods of receiving a reward, which is not only much more efficient and effective when teaching boundaries, rewards are far kinder, and create a much stronger bond with your dog.

### a) The Truth About Shock Collars

First of all, it would have to be an extremely rare situation in which it would be necessary or recommended that you use a shock collar on a Australian Labradoodle as these devices are usually only employed in extreme situations, and generally for much larger breeds who could seriously harm someone.

The use of remote, electronic, shock or *"e-collars"* is at best a controversial subject that can quickly escalate into heated arguments.

In certain, rare circumstances, and when used correctly, the e-collar can be a helpful training tool that could actually save a dog's life if they are acting out in dangerous ways that could seriously harm or even kill them.

An e-collar would generally be utilized in a circumstance where a larger breed of dog has access to free range over a large property, resulting in difficulties getting their attention from a distance if they become distracted by other animals or smells.

Many dogs that have not been properly trained from a young age also learn that when they are off leash and out of your immediate reach that they can choose to ignore your commands, bark their heads off, terrorize the neighbors or chase wildlife.

All of these situations are generally not activities that a Australian Labradoodle would have the slightest interest in, unless they have access to a large property and their hunting instinct kicks in, because they would prefer being at home with their humans.

Generally e-collars can be effective training tools for working breed herding, hunting or tracking dogs.

In these types of circumstances a remote training collar can be an effective training device for reinforcing verbal commands from a great distance, such as “Come”, “Sit” or “Stay”.

Finally, electronic collars can be used as a last resort to help teach a dog not to engage in a dangerous behavior that could result in them being seriously harmed or even killed.

**b) Electronic Fencing**

Honestly, there are far more reasons NOT to install an electronic fence as a means of keeping your dog inside your yard, than there are good reasons for considering one.

In most cases, humans who install electronic fencing because they are worried that their dog will run away have simply not taken the time to develop a relationship of trust and respect with their canine companion.

For instance, a dog whose yard is surrounded by an electronic fence can quite easily develop fear, aggression, or both, directed toward what they may believe is the cause of the shock they are receiving.

As a result, installing an electronic fence may cause your Australian Labradoodle to become aggressive toward cats, other dogs, other humans, other wildlife, children riding by on bikes or skateboards, the mail carrier, or the people next door.

As well, a dog that receives a fright, or in excitement forgets about the shock they are going to receive, may run through an electronic fence and then be too frightened or stressed to come back home because it means that they must pass through the painful barrier again.

Further, it is actually possible that electronic fencing may encourage a dog to escape the yard simply because they associate their yard with pain. This feeling can be reinforced if a dog escapes the electronic yard and then is again punished by the shock when they attempt to come home.

Another factor to keep in mind with respect to electronic fencing is that other dogs or teasing children can freely enter the yard and torment or attack your dog, and a thief bent on stealing your Australian Labradoodle will be able to do so with ease.

The absolute best way to keep your dog safe in their own yard, while helping to establish your role as guardian and leader, is to be out there with them while they are on leash, and to only permit them freedom in your yard under your close supervision.

# Chapter 11: Medical Care & Safety

## 1. Choosing a Veterinarian

A consideration to keep in mind when choosing a veterinarian clinic will be that some clinics specialize in caring for smaller pets, and some specialize in larger animal care, while still others have a wide ranging area of expertise and will care for all animals, including livestock and reptiles.

Choosing a clinic will be a personal decision, however, since the Australian Labradoodle is considered a smaller breed of dog, your dog's needs may be better served by choosing a clinic that specializes in the care of smaller pets.

Choosing a good veterinary clinic will be very similar to choosing the right health care clinic or doctor for your own personal health because you want to ensure that your Australian Labradoodle puppy receives the quality care they deserve.

Begin your search by asking other dog owners where they take their fur friends and whether they are happy with the service they receive.

If you don't know anyone to ask, visit the local pet store in your area as they should be able to provide you with references and local listings of pet care clinics.

Next, check online, because a good pet clinic will have an active website up and running that will list details of all the services they provide along with an overview of all staff members, their education and qualifications.

Once you've narrowed your search, it's time to personally visit the clinics you may be interested in, as this will be a good opportunity for you to visually inspect the facility, interact with the staff and perhaps meet the veterinarians face to face.

Of course, it's not just you who needs to feel comfortable with the clinic chosen and those working there. Your puppy needs to feel comfortable, too, and this is where visiting a clinic and interacting with the staff and veterinarians will provide you with an idea of their experience and expertise in handling your puppy.

If your puppy is comfortable with them, then you will be much more likely to trust that they will be providing the best care for your puppy who will need to receive all their vaccinations and yearly check-ups, and eventually be spayed or neutered.

It's also a good idea to take your puppy into your chosen clinic several times before they actually need to be there for any treatment, so that they are not fearful of the new smells and unfamiliar surroundings.

## 2. Neutering and Spaying

While it can sometimes be difficult to find the definitive answer when asking when is the best time to neuter or spay your young Australian Labradoodle, because there are varying opinions on this topic, one thing that most veterinarians do agree on is that earlier spaying or neutering, between 4 and 6 months of age, is a better choice than waiting. Spaying or neutering surgeries are carried out under general anesthesia, and as more dogs are being neutered at younger ages, speak with your veterinarian and ask for their recommendations regarding the right age to spay or neuter your Australian Labradoodle.

### a) Effects on Aggression

Intact (non-neutered) males and females are more likely to display aggression related to sexual behavior than are dogs that have been neutered or spayed.

Fighting, particularly in male dogs that is directed at other males, is less common after neutering, and the intensity of other types of aggression, such as irritable aggression in females will be totally eliminated by spaying.

While neutering or spaying is not a treatment for aggression, it can certainly help to minimize the severity and escalation of aggressiveness and is often the first step toward resolving an aggressive behavior problem.

**b) What is Neutering?**

Neutering is a surgical procedure, carried out by a licensed veterinarian surgeon to render a male dog unable to reproduce.

In males, the surgery is also referred to as *"castration"* because the procedure entails the removal of the young dog's testicles. When the testicles are removed, what is left behind is an empty scrotal sac (which used to contain the puppy's testicles) and this empty sac will soon shrink in size until it is no longer noticeable.

**c) Neutering Males**

Neutering male Australian Labradoodle puppies before they are six months of age can help to ensure that they will be less likely to suffer from obesity problems when they grow older.

Neutering can also mean that a male Australian Labradoodle will be less likely to have the urge to wander.

Further, waiting until a male Australian Labradoodle is older than six months before having them neutered could mean that they will experience the effects of raging testosterone that will drive them to escape their yards by any means necessary to search out females to mate with.

Non-neutered males also tend to spray or mark territory much more often, both inside and outside the home, and during this time can start to display aggressive tendencies toward other dogs as well as people.

## d) What is Spaying?

In female puppies, sterilization, referred to as *"spaying"* is a surgical procedure carried out by a licensed veterinarian, to prevent the female dog from becoming pregnant and to stop regular heat cycles.

The sterilization procedure is much more involved for a female puppy (than for a male), as it requires the removal of both ovaries and the uterus by incision into the puppy's abdominal cavity. The uterus is also removed during this surgery, to prevent the possibility of it becoming infected later on in life.

## e) Spaying Females

Preferably, female Australian Labradoodle puppies should be spayed before their very first estrus or heat cycle. Females in heat often appear more agitated and irritable, while sleeping and eating less and some may become extremely aggressive toward other dogs.

Spaying female puppies before their first heat pattern can eliminate these hormonal stressors and reduce the opportunity of mammary glandular tumors. Early spaying also protects against various other potential concerns, such as uterine infections.

## f) Effects on General Temperament

Many dog owners often become needlessly worried that a neutered or spayed dog will lose their vigor.
Rest assured that a dog's personality or energy level will not be modified or altered in any way by the neutering process, and in fact, many unfavorable qualities resulting from hormonal impact may resolve after surgery.

Your Australian Labradoodle will certainly not come to be less caring or cheerful, and neither will he or she resent you because you are not denying your dog any essential encounters. You will, however, be acting as a conscientious, informed, and caring Australian Labradoodle guardian.

Further, there is little evidence to suggest that the nature of a female Australian Labradoodle will improve after having a litter of puppies.

What is important is that you do not project your own psychological needs or concerns onto your Australian Labradoodle puppy, because there is no gain to be had from permitting sexual activity in either male or female canines.

For instance, it is not *"abnormal"* or *"mean"* to manage a puppy's reproductive activity by having them sterilized. Rather, it is unkind and irresponsible not to neuter or spay a dog and there are many positive benefits of having this procedure carried out.

**g) Effects on Escape and Roaming**

A neutered or spayed Australian Labradoodle is less likely to wander. Castrated male dogs have the tendency to patrol smaller sized outdoor areas and are less likely to participate in territorial conflicts with perceived opponents.

NOTE: an Australian Labradoodle that has actually already experienced successful escapes from the yard may continue to wander after they are spayed or neutered.

**h) Effects on Problem Elimination**

An unsterilized dog may urinate or defecate inside the home or in other undesirable areas in an attempt to stake territorial claims, relieve anxiety, or advertise their available reproductive status.

While neutering or spaying a Australian Labradoodle puppy after they have already begun to inappropriately eliminate or mark territory to announce their sexual availability to other dogs will reduce the more powerful urine odor as well as eliminate the hormonal factors, once this habit has begun, the undesirable behavior may continue to persist after neutering or spaying.

### i) Possible Weight Gain

While metabolic changes that occur after spaying or neutering can cause some Australian Labradoodle puppy's to gain weight, often the real culprit for any weight gain is the human who feels guilty for subjecting their puppy to any kind of pain and therefore, they attempt to make themselves feel better by feeding more treats or meals to their Australian Labradoodle companion.

If you are concerned about weight gain after neutering or spaying a Australian Labradoodle puppy, simply adjust their food and treat consumption, as needed, and make sure that they receive adequate daily exercise.

It's a very simply process to change your Australian Labradoodle's food intake according to their physical demands and how they look, and if your Australian Labradoodle puppy's daily exercise and level of activity has not changed after they have been spayed or neutered, there will likely be no change in food management necessary.

### j) Pediatric Spaying/Neutering

In the past, the usual time frame for neutering or spaying a puppy was between the ages of 5 and 6 months. However, even though there exists quite a bit of debate amongst veterinarians, pediatric spaying or neutering has become more widely accepted.
The American Veterinary Medical Association has supported this concept of very early sterilization since 2004 in an effort to help reduce the numbers of homeless, unwanted animals.

Pediatric spaying or neutering is also called *"prepuberal"* or "early" spaying or neutering and may be carried out at a much earlier age, usually between 6 and 14 weeks.

## 3. Why Vaccinate a Puppy?

Puppies need to be vaccinated by a veterinarian in order to provide them with protection against four common and serious diseases.
Vaccination against this common set of diseases is referred to as *"DAPP"*, which stands for Distemper, Adenovirus, Parainfluenza and Parvo Virus.

Approximate one week after your Australian Labradoodle puppy has completed all three sets of primary DAPP vaccinations they will be fully protected from those specific diseases. Thereafter, most veterinarians will recommend a once a year vaccination for the next year or two.

It has now become common practice to vaccinate adult dogs every three years, and if your veterinarian is insisting on a yearly vaccination for your Australian Labradoodle puppy, you need to ask them why, because to do otherwise is considered by most professionals to be *"over vaccinating"*.

**a) Distemper**

Canine distemper is a contagious and serious viral illness for which there is currently no known cure.

This deadly virus, which is spread either through the air or by direct or indirect contact with a dog that is already infected, or other distemper carrying wildlife, including ferrets, raccoons, foxes, skunks and wolves, is a relative of the measles virus which affects humans.

Canine distemper is sometimes also called *"hard pad disease"* because some strains of the distemper virus actually cause thickening of the pads on a dog's feet, which can also affect the end of a dog's nose.

In dogs or animals with weak immune systems, death may result two to five weeks after the initial distemper infection.

Early symptoms of distemper include fever, loss of appetite, and mild eye inflammation that may only last a day or two. Symptoms become more serious and noticeable as the disease progresses.

A puppy or dog that survives the distemper virus will usually continue to experience symptoms or signs of the disease throughout their remaining lifespan, including *"hard pad disease"* as well as *"enamel hypoplasia"*, which is damage to the enamel of the puppy's teeth that are not yet formed or that have not yet pushed through the gums.

Enamel hypoplasia is caused when the distemper virus kills the cells that manufacture tooth enamel.

**b) Adenovirus**

Is a virus that causes infectious canine hepatitis, which can range in severity from very mild to very serious, sometimes resulting in death.

Symptoms can include coughing, loss of appetite, increased thirst and urination, tiredness, runny eyes and nose, vomiting, bruising or bleeding under the skin, swelling of the head, neck and body, fluid accumulation in the abdomen area, jaundice (yellow tinge to the skin), a bluish clouding of the cornea of the eye (called "hepatitis blue eye") and seizures.

There is no specific treatment for infectious canine hepatitis. Treatment of the disease is focused on managing symptoms while the virus runs its course. Hospitalization and intravenous fluid therapy may be required in severe cases.

**c) Canine Parainfluenza Virus**

The canine parainfluenza virus (CPIV) also referred to as *"canine influenza virus"*, *"greyhound disease"* or *"race flu"*, which is easily spread through the air or by coming into contact with respiratory secretions, was originally a virus that only affected horses.

This disease is believed to have adapted to become contagious to dogs, is easily spread from dog to dog, and may cause symptoms that become fatal.

While the more frequent occurrences of this respiratory infection are seen in areas where there are high dog populations, such as race tracks, boarding kennels and pet stores, this virus is highly contagious to any dog or puppy, at any age.

Symptoms can include a dry, hacking cough, difficulty breathing, wheezing, runny nose and eyes, sneezing, fever, loss of appetite, tiredness, depression and possible pneumonia.

In cases where only a cough exists, tests will be required to determine whether the cause of the cough is the parainfluenza virus or the less serious *"kennel cough"*.

While many dogs can naturally recover from this virus, they will remain contagious, and for this reason, in order to prevent the spread to other animals, aggressive treatment of the virus, with antibiotics and antiviral drugs will be the general course of action.

In more severe cases, a cough suppressant may be prescribed, as well as intravenous fluids to help prevent secondary bacterial infection.

**d) Canine Parvovirus**

Canine parvovirus (CPV) is a highly contagious viral illness affecting puppies and dogs. Parvovirus also affects other canine species including foxes, coyotes and wolves.

There are two forms of this virus (1) the more common intestinal form, and (2) the less common cardiac form, which can cause death in young puppies.

Symptoms of the intestinal form of parvovirus include vomiting, bloody diarrhea, weight loss, and lack of appetite, while the less common cardiac form attacks the heart muscle.

Early vaccination in young puppies has radically reduced the incidence of canine parvovirus infection, which is easily transmitted either by direct contact with an infected dog, or indirectly, by sniffing an infected dog's feces.

The virus can also be brought into a dog's environment on the bottom of human shoes that may have stepped on infected feces, and there is evidence that this hardy virus can live in ground soil for up to a year. Recovery from parvovirus requires both aggressive and early treatment. With proper treatment, death rates are relatively low (between 5 and 20%), although chances of survival for puppies are much lower than for older dogs, and in all instances, there is no guarantee of survival.

Treatment of parvovirus requires hospitalization where intravenous fluids and nutrients are administered to help combat dehydration. As well, antibiotics will be given to counteract secondary bacterial infections, and as necessary, medications to control nausea and vomiting may also be given.

Without prompt and proper treatment, dogs that have severe parvovirus infections can die within 48 to 72 hours.

## 4. Other Diseases and Viruses

### a) Rabies Vaccinations

Rabies is a viral disease transmitted by coming into contact with the saliva of an infected animal, usually through a bite.

The virus travels to the brain along the nerves and once symptoms develop, death is almost certainly inevitable, usually following a prolonged period of suffering.

If you plan to travel out of State or across country borders, you will need to make sure that your Australian Labradoodle has an up to date Rabies Vaccination Certificate (NASPHV form 51) indicating they have been inoculated against rabies.

Vaccinating dogs against rabies is also compulsory in most countries in mainland Europe, as is permanent identification and registration of dogs through the use of a Pet Passport.

Those living in a country that is rabies free (UK, Eire) are not required to vaccinate their dogs against rabies, unless they intend to travel.

**b) Leishmaniasis**

Leishmaniasis is caused by a parasite and is transmitted by a bite from a sand fly.

There is no definitive answer for effectively combating Leishmaniasis, especially since one vaccine will not prevent the known multiple species.

In areas where the known cause is a sand fly, deltamethrin collars (containing a neurotoxic insecticide) worn by the dogs has been proven to be 86% effective.

There are two types of Leishmaniasis: (1) a skin reaction causing hair loss, lesions and ulcerative dermatitis, and (2) a more severe, abdominal organ reaction, which is also known as *"black fever"*. When the disease affects organs of the abdominal cavity the symptoms include:

- Loss of appetite
- Diarrhea

- Severe weight loss
- Exercise intolerance
- Vomiting
- Nose bleed
- Tarry feces
- Fever
- Pain in the joints
- Excessive thirst and urination
- Inflammation of the muscles

Leishmaniasis spreads throughout the body to most organs, with kidney failure being the most common cause of death. Virtually all infected dogs develop this system wide disease and as much as 90% of those infected will also display skin reactions.

Affected dogs in the US are frequently found to have acquired this infection in another country.

Of note, is that this disease is regularly found in the Middle East, the area around the Mediterranean basin, Portugal, Spain, Africa, South and Central America, southern Mexico and the US, with regular cases reported in Oklahoma and Ohio, where it is found in 20 to 40% of the dog population.

There have also been a few reported cases in Switzerland, northern France and the Netherlands.

NOTE: Leishmaniasis is a *"zoonotic"* infection, which is a contagious disease that can be spread between both animals and humans.
This means that the organisms residing in the Leishmaniasis lesions can be communicated to humans.

Treatment in dogs is often difficult and the dog may suffer from relapses. Leishmaniasis poses a significant risk to the health of your dog, especially if you travel to the Mediterranean.

### c) Lyme Disease

This is one of the most common tick-borne diseases in the world, which is transmitted by Borrelia bacteria found in the deer or sheep tick.

Lyme disease, also called *"borreliosis"*, is also a zoonotic disease that can affect both humans and dogs and this disease can be fatal.

The Borrelia bacteria that causes Lyme's disease, is transmitted by slow-feeding, hard-shelled deer or sheep ticks, and the tick usually has to be attached to the dog for a minimum of 18 hours before the infection is transmitted.

Symptoms of this disease in a young or adult dog include:

- Recurrent lameness from joint inflammation
- Loss of appetite
- Depression
- Stiff walk with arched back
- Sensitivity to touch
- Swollen lymph nodes
- Fever
- Kidney damage
- Rare heart or nervous system complications

While Lyme disease has been reported in dogs throughout the United States and Europe, it is most prevalent in the upper Mid-Western states, the Atlantic seaboard, and the Pacific coastal states.
In order to properly diagnose and treat Lyme disease, blood tests will be required, and if the tests are positive, oral antibiotics will be prescribed to treat the conditions.

Prevention is the key to keeping this disease under control because dogs that have had Lyme disease before are still able to get the disease again.

There is a vaccine for Lyme disease and dogs living in areas that have easy access to these ticks should be vaccinated yearly.

**d) Rocky Mountain Spotted Fever**

This tick-transmitted disease is very often seen in dogs in the East, Midwest, and plains region of the US, and the organisms causing Rocky Mountain Spotted Fever (RMSF) are transmitted by both the American dog tick and the RMSF tick, which must be attached to the dog for a minimum of five hours in order to transmit the disease.

Common symptoms of RMSF include:

- Fever
- Reduced appetite
- Depression
- Pain in the joints
- Lameness
- Vomiting
- Diarrhea

Some dogs affected with RMSF may develop heart abnormalities, pneumonia, kidney failure, liver damage, or even neurological signs, such an seizures or unsteady, wobbly or stumbling gait.

Diagnosis of this disease requires blood testing and if the results are positive, oral antibiotics will be given to the infected dog for approximately two weeks.

Dogs that can clear the organism from their systems will recover and after being infected, will remain immune to future infection.

**e) Ehrlichiosis**

This is another tick borne disease transmitted by both the brown dog tick and the Lone Star Tick.

Ehrlichiosis has been reported in every state in the US, as well as worldwide. Common symptoms include:

- Depression
- Reduced appetite
- Fever
- Stiff and painful joints
- Bruising

Signs of infection typically occur less than a month after a tick bite and last for approximately four weeks. There is no vaccine available.

Blood tests may be required to test for antibodies and treatment will require a course of antibiotics for up to four weeks in order to completely clear the organism from the infected dog's system.

After a dog has been previously infected, they may develop antibodies to the organism, but will not be immune to being re-infected.

Dogs living in areas of the country where the Ehrlichiosis tick disease are common or widespread may be prescribed low doses of antibiotics during tick season.

**f) Anaplasmosis**

Deer ticks and Western blacklegged ticks are carriers of the bacteria that transmit canine Anaplasmosis.

However, there is also another form of Anaplasmosis (caused by a different bacteria) that is carried by the brown dog tick. Because the deer tick also carries other diseases, some animals may be at risk for developing more than one tick-borne disease at the same time.

Signs of Anaplasmosis are similar to Ehrlichiosis and include painful joints, diarrhea, fever, and vomiting as well as possible nervous system disorders.

A dog will usually begin to show signs of Anaplasmosis within a couple of weeks after infection and diagnosis will require blood and urine testing, and sometimes other specialized laboratory tests.

Treatment is with oral antibiotics for up to 30 days, depending on how severe the infection may be.

When this disease is quickly treated, most dogs will recover completely, however, subsequent immunity is not guaranteed, which means that a dog may be re-infected if exposed again.

**g) Tick Paralysis**

Tick paralysis is caused when ticks secrete a toxin that affects the nervous system.

Affected dogs show signs of weakness and limpness approximately one week after being first bitten by ticks.

Symptoms usual begin with a change in pitch of the dog's usual bark, which will become softer, and weakness in the rear legs that eventually involves all four legs, which is then followed by the dog showing difficulty breathing and swallowing. If the condition is not diagnosed and properly treated, death can occur.

Treatment involves locating and removing the tick and then treating the infected dog with tick anti-serum.

**h) Canine Coronavirus**

While this highly contagious intestinal disease, which is spread through the feces of contaminated dogs, was first discovered in

Germany during 1971 when there was an outbreak in sentry dogs, it is now found worldwide.

This virus can be destroyed by most commonly available disinfectants.

Symptoms include:

- Diarrhea
- Vomiting
- Weight loss or anorexia

While deaths resulting from this disease are rare, and treatment generally requires only medication to relieve the diarrhea, dogs that are more severely affected may require intravenous fluids to combat dehydration.

There is a vaccine available, which is usually given to puppies, because they are more susceptible at a young age. This vaccine is also given to show dogs that have a higher risk of exposure to the disease.

**i) Leptospirosis**

This is a disease that occurs throughout the world that can affect many different kinds of animals, including dogs, and as it is also a zoonotic disease, this means that it can affect humans, too. There is potential for both dogs and humans to die from this disease. The disease is always present in the environment, which makes it easy for any dog to pick up. This is because it is found in many common animals, such as rats, and wildlife, as well as domestic livestock.

Veterinarians generally see more cases of Leptospirosis in the late summer and fall, which is probably because that is when more pets and wildlife are out and about.

More cases also occur after heavy rain falls.

The disease is most common in mild or tropical climates around the World, and in the US or Canada, it is more common in states or provinces that receive heavy rainfall.

The good news is that you can protect your dog from leptospirosis by vaccination, and while puppies are not routinely vaccinated against leptospirosis because chances of contracting the disease depends upon the lifestyle of the dog as well as the area in which the dog lives, it makes sense to vaccinate against this disease if you and your dog do live in an area considered a hot spot for leptospirosis, so ask your veterinarian.

City rat populations are a major carrier of leptospirosis.

Cold winter conditions lower the risk because the leptospira organisms do not tolerate the freezing and thawing of near-zero temperatures. They are killed rapidly by drying, but they persist in standing water, dampness, mud and alkaline conditions.

Most of the infected wild animals and domestic animals that spread leptospirosis do not appear ill.

The leptospira take up residence in the kidneys of infected animals, which can include rats, mice, squirrels, skunks, and raccoons and when these animals void urine, they contaminate their environment with living leptospira.

Dogs usually become infected after sniffing urine or by wading, swimming or drinking contaminated water that has infected urine in it, and this is how the disease passes from animal to animal. As well, the leptospira can also enter through a bite wound or if a dog eats infected material.

## 5. Additional Vaccinations

Depending upon where you and your Australian Labradoodle live, your veterinarian may suggest additional vaccinations to help combat diseases that may be more common in your area.

## 6. When Is a Puppy Vaccinated?

The first vaccination needle is normally given to a puppy around six to eight weeks of age, which means that generally it will be the responsibility of the Australian Labradoodle breeder to ensure that the puppy's first shots have been received before their new owner takes them home.

Thereafter, it will be the new Australian Labradoodle puppy's guardians that will be responsible for ensuring that the next two sets of shots, which are usually given three to four weeks after each other, are given by the new guardian's veterinarian at the proper intervals.

## 7. De-Worming

De-worming kills internal parasites that your dog or puppy may have. The two most common types of worms that may infest your canine companion are round worms and tapeworms, both of which can be passed on to humans.

NOTE: even though your living conditions may be completely sanitary, it is still possible for your dog to have internal parasites because this has nothing to do with where you live or how clean you keep your dog and your home.
It is recommended by the Center for Disease Control (CDC) that puppies be dewormed every 2 weeks until they are 3 months old, and then every month after that, in order to control worms.

Even though puppies are usually regularly wormed by the breeder before the puppies are taken to their forever homes, many veterinarians recommend regularly worming dogs for tapeworm and roundworms every 6-12 months.

The health risk to your puppy or dog includes diarrhea, vomiting, slow growth, and in serious cases causing a bowel blockage or pneumonia, even death.

Most all puppies and dogs will experience worms at some stage in their life and thankfully the problem can be easily and swiftly eliminated with worming medication.

## 8. Special Care When Pregnant

As canine pregnancy lasts approximately 63 days, and an Australian Labradoodle female will go into labor within 56 to 66 days after becoming pregnant, a pregnant Australian Labradoodle will require immediate attention when the first signs of pregnancy appear.

Immediately upon noticing signs of pregnancy you will want to take your Australian Labradoodle to your veterinarian to confirm the pregnancy and to receive instructions for the proper feeding and care.

During the first days of pregnancy your Australian Labradoodle may experience morning sickness.

Your veterinarian may recommend increasing food intake or adding an egg or cottage cheese to your Australian Labradoodle's meals and switching to puppy kibble, which is higher in protein, at around the 30 day mark.
As the Australian Labradoodle female becomes heavier with the puppies, she will lose interest in exercising and her other normal activities and will need to sleep more.

When the time for birthing is drawing near, the Australian Labradoodle female will start to display "nesting" characteristics where she will search for a warm and safe place to give birth.

You can help by providing a nesting box and she will likely want to take things into the box to make it more comfortable, such as towels or even a stuffed toy that she will begin to mother.

When the time draws near to whelping, the Australian Labradoodle female may completely lose her appetite and show distress by pacing, panting, and acting uncomfortable.
When the birthing time is near, the dog's temperature needs to be checked, and should be around 100.2 to 100.8 degrees Fahrenheit (37.89 to 38.22 degrees Centigrade).

When her temperature drops to approximately 98 to 99.4 degrees Fahrenheit (36.67 to 37.44 degrees Centigrade), the puppies will usually be born within 24 hours.

If you are at all worried about the birthing process you will want to take the mother Australian Labradoodle immediately to your veterinarian's office.

If all goes well at home, within 5-6 hours of the last puppy's birth, you will need to take the mother and her puppies to your veterinarian for a check up to make sure that she has birthed all puppies and placentas, and that the puppies are all healthy.

## 9. Licensing

Many cities and jurisdictions around the world require that dogs be licensed.

Usually a dog license is an identifying tag that the dog will be required to wear on their collar. The tag will have an identifying number and a contact number for the registering organization, so that if someone finds a lost dog wearing a tag, the owner of the dog can be contacted.

Most dog tags are only valid for one year, and will need to be renewed annually at the beginning of every New Year, which involves paying a fee, which can vary from jurisdiction to jurisdiction.

From one extreme to the next, owners of dogs living in Beijing, China must pay a licensing fee of $600 (£360), while those living in Great Britain require no fee, because licensing of dogs was abolished in 1987.

Ireland and Northern Ireland both require dogs to be licensed and in Germany dog ownership is taxed, rather than requiring licensing, with higher taxes being paid for breeds of dogs deemed to be “dangerous”.

Most US states and municipalities have licensing laws in effect and Canadian, Australian and New Zealand dogs also must be licensed, with the yearly fee approximately $30 to $50 (£18 to £30) depending upon whether the dog has been spayed or neutered.

## 10. Pet Insurance

Pet guardians commonly ask themselves, when considering medical insurance for their dog, whether they can afford <u>not</u> to have it.

On the one hand, in light of all the new treatments and medications that are now available for our dogs, that usually come with a very high price tag, an increasing number of guardians have decided to add pet insurance to their list of monthly expenses.
On the other hand, some humans believe that placing money into a savings account, in case unforeseen medical treatments are required, makes more sense.

Pet insurance coverage can cost anywhere from $2,000 to $6,000 USD (£1,201 to £3,604) over an average lifespan of a dog, and unless your dog is involved in a serious accident, or contracts a life-threatening disease, you may never need to pay out that much for treatment.

Whether you decide to start a savings account for your Australian Labradoodle so that you will always have funds available for unforeseen health issues, or you decide to buy a health insurance plan, most dog lovers will go to any lengths to save the life of their beloved companions.

Having access to advanced technological tools and procedures means that our dogs are now being offered treatment options that were once only reserved for humans.

Now, some canine conditions that were once considered fatal, are being treated at considerable costs ranging anywhere between $1,000 and $5,000 (£597 and £2,986) or more.

However, even in the face of rapidly increasing costs of caring for our dogs, owners purchasing pet insurance remain a small minority.

In an effort to increase the numbers of people buying pet insurance, insurers have teamed with the American Kennel Club and Petco Animal Supplies to offer the insurance, and more than 1,600 companies, such as Office Depot and Google, offer pet insurance coverage to their employees as an optional employee benefit.

Even though you might believe that pet insurance will be your savior anytime your dog needs a trip to the vet's office, you really need to be careful when considering an insurance plan, because there are many policies that contain small print excluding certain ages, hereditary or chronic conditions.

Unfortunately, most people don't consider pet insurance when their pets are healthy because buying pet insurance means playing the odds, and unless your dog becomes seriously ill, you end up paying for something that may never happen.

However, just like automobile insurance, you can't buy it after you've had that accident.

For instance, if you take your dog to your veterinarian who discovers that they have something wrong with their eyes, and then you decide to purchase insurance, because you will be required to give the insuring company a history of your dog's health, the eye issue will be part of the history and will likely be excluded from your insurance policy.

In other words, if you're planning on purchasing health insurance for your dog, do it before any problems arise in order to avoid having conditions that may present themselves in the future from being excluded from your policy.

As well, you need to keep in mind that canine health insurance rates will likely increase as your dog becomes older. When your dog is younger, while your policy may only be $17 (£10) per month, it may increase considerably to as much as $170 (£100) or more per month as your dog becomes middle or senior aged, at around 8 to 10 years of age.

Since many of us, in today's uncertain economy, may be hard pressed to pay a high veterinarian bill, generally speaking, the alternative of paying monthly pet insurance premiums will provide peace of mind and improved veterinarian care for our best friends.

Shop around, because as with all insurance policies, pet insurance policies will vary greatly between companies and the only way to know for certain exactly what sort of coverage you are buying is to be holding a copy of that policy in your hand so that you can clearly read what will and what will not be covered.
Don't forget to carefully read the fine print to avoid any nasty surprises, because the time to discover that a certain procedure will not be covered is not when you are in the middle of filing a claim.

**Before Purchasing a Policy**

There are several considerations to be aware of before choosing to purchase a pet insurance policy, including:

- Is your dog required to undergo a physical exam?
- Is there a waiting period before the policy becomes active?
- What percentage of the bill does the insurance company pay — after the deductible?
- Are payments limited or capped in any way?
- Are there co-pays (cost to you up front)?
- Does the plan cover pre-existing conditions?
- Does the plan cover chronic or recurring medical problems?
- Can you choose any vet or animal hospital to treat your pet?
- Are prescription medications covered?
- Are you covered when traveling with your pet?
- Does the policy pay if your pet is being treated and then dies?

When you love your dog and worry that you may not have the funds to cover an emergency medical situation that could unexpectedly cost thousands, the right pet insurance policy will provide both peace of mind and better health care for your beloved fur friend.

## 11. Identifying and Finding Lost Dogs

### a) Micro-Chipping

A microchip implant is a very small integrated circuit, approximately twice the size of a grain of rice, enclosed in glass that is implanted underneath the dog's skin (or other animal) with a syringe.

The chip uses passive Radio Frequency Identification (RFID) technology, and is also known as a PIT tag (Passive Integrated Transponder).

The microchip is usually implanted, without anesthetic, into the scruff of a dog's neck by a veterinarian or shelter.

The microchip has no internal power source, which means that they must be read by a scanner or *"interrogator"* which energizes the capacitor in the chip, which then sends radio signals back to the scanner so that the identifying number can be read.

Manufacturers of microchips often donate scanners to animal shelters and veterinarian clinics and hospitals.

While many communities are proposing making micro-chipping of all dogs mandatory, such as N. Ireland, and micro-chipping is a requirements for any dogs traveling to the state of Hawaii, many others are not especially pleased with this idea because they believe it's just more big business for little reward.

For instance, while approximately one quarter of European dogs have a microchip implant, the idea is definitely lacking in popularity in the United States, where only 5% of dogs are micro-chipped.

Even though micro-chipping is used by animal shelters, pounds, animal control officers, breeders and veterinarians, in order to help return a higher percentage of lost canines to their owners, some of the resistance to this idea can be explained by inherent problems with the ability of some organizations to correctly read the implants.

As an example, if the scanner is not tuned to the same frequency as the implanted microchip, it will not be read, which renders the process useless.

Pet microchips are manufactured with different frequencies, including 125 kHz, 128 kHz and 134.2 kHz.

While approximately 98% of the pet microchips in the US use 125 kHz, those in Europe use 134.2 kHz.

In other words, if the facility reading your dog's microchip does not have a compatible scanner, your dog will not be identified and returned to you.

Further, what may turn out to be worse than the scanner incompatibility problem could be increasing evidence to indicate that microchips might cause cancer.

As well some microchips will migrate inside the dog's body and while they may start out in the dogs neck, they could end up in their leg or some other body part.

You will have to weigh information known about microchips, including possible cancer risks, and the odds of losing your dog against whether or not a microchip is something you want to have for your Australian Labradoodle.

Whether or not you choose a microchip for your dog, generally the cost ranges between $25 and $50 (£15 and £30) depending on what your veterinarian may charge for this service.

**b) Tattooing**

Dogs are tattooed to help identify them in case they are lost or stolen and many dog guardians prefer this safe, simple solution to micro-chipping.

Tattooing does not require locating a scanner that reads the correct frequency and there are no known side effects.

Because a tattoo is visible, it is immediately recognizable and reported when a lost dog is found, which means that tattooing could easily be the most effective means of identification available.

As well, dog thieves are less likely to steal a dog that has a permanent visible form of identification. There are several registries for tattooed dogs, including the National Dog Tattoo

Registry in the UK, which has a network of Accredited Tattooists across the UK.

The fee for tattooing and registering a dog for their lifetime is approximately $42.52 (£24.98).

In the United States, the National Dog Registry (NDR) was founded in 1966 and since then, NDR has supervised, directed, conducted, or overseen the tattooing of more than 6 million animals.

The cost for tattooing a single dog is approximately $10 (£5.90), and you will also have to pay a one-time registration fee of $45 (£26.44).

**c) Where to Look**

If your Australian Labradoodle goes missing, there are many places you can contact and steps you can take that may help you locate your lost dog, including:

- Retracing your dog's last known location;
- Contacting your friends and neighbours;
- Putting up flyers on telephone poles throughout your neighbourhood, with your contact details and a photograph of your dog;
- Calling all local shelters and pounds every day;
- Contacting local rescue organisations;
- Contacting your breeder;
- Contacting local schools -- children might have seen your dog in their neighbourhood;
- Distributing flyers with a photograph of your dog and your contact details in all neighbourhood stores and businesses;

- Contacting all businesses that deal with lost pets;
- Posting a picture on your Facebook or other social media;
- Asking your local radio station for help;
- Advertising in your local newspaper.

## 12. Yearly Cost of Ownership

It can be difficult to accurately estimate what the cost of owning every Australian Labradoodle might be because there are too many variables and unexpected medical problems, which might arise that may not otherwise be considered average.

For instance, you may like to buy fancy clothes, new collars and leashes every year, the latest toys and gadgets, or the most expensive food for your dog every week that might also not be considered average.

However, when thinking about sharing your life with a dog, it's important to consider more than just the daily cost of feeding your Australian Labradoodle.

Many humans do not think about whether or not they can truly afford to care for a dog before they bring one home, and not being prepared can cause stress and problems later on.

Remember that being financially responsible for your Australian Labradoodle is a large part of being a good guardian.

Beyond the initial investment of purchasing your Australian Labradoodle puppy from a reputable breeder, for most guardians, owning an Australian Labradoodle will include the costs associated with the following:

- Food
- Treats
- Pee pads, poop bags, potty patches

- Leashes and collars
- Safety harnesses
- Travel kennels or bags
- House training pens
- Clothing
- Toys
- Beds
- Professional grooming or equipment
- Shampoo and conditioner
- Neutering or spaying
- Regular veterinary care
- Obedience or dog whispering classes
- Pet sitting, walking or boarding
- Pet insurance
- Tattooing
- Micro-chipping
- Yearly licensing
- Unexpected emergencies

As you can see from the list above, there are many variables involved with being a canine guardian that may or may not apply to your particular situation.

For instance, depending upon where you shop, what type of food and how much you feed your Australian Labradoodle, what sort of veterinarian or grooming care you choose, whether or not you have pet insurance and what types of items you purchase for your Australian Labradoodle's well being, the yearly cost of owning a Australian Labradoodle could be estimated at anywhere between $700 and $3,000 (£420 and £1,800).

Other contributing factors that may have an effect on the overall yearly cost of owning a Australian Labradoodle can include the region where you live, the weather, the accessibility of the items you need, your own lifestyle preferences and your Australian Labradoodle's age and individual needs.

NOTE: another interesting fact that may influence the overall cost associated with caring for a particular breed of dog is, according to a recent study of 2,000 dogs, closely related to what breed of dog you may be sharing your home with.

According to a recent article written by Sarah Griffiths and published in the Daily Mail on June 13, 2014, there is now a list of the top ten most *"destructive"* purebred dog breeds.

This interesting study was carried out in reference to damage a dog may cause by ripping up the carpet, chewing through the fence, destroying the plants in the garden, eating the remote or your most expensive shoes, etc.

Of course, all us humans expect some degree of damage from our furry friends during their lifetime, however, sometimes it can be quite a surprisingly large amount when you begin to add up the total amounts spent on cleaning, replacing and repairing damaged property, and the amount can be even higher if your dog becomes involved in destroying the neighbor's property, too.

The prize for the top ten destroyers is awarded to the cute and tiny Chihuahua, with average repair costs totaling $1,468 (£866) over the dog's lifetime, followed by the Dachshund, Dalmatian, Bulldog, Great Dane, Husky, Beagle, Pointer and German Shepherd.

On the other hand, the top ten least destructive breeds, in descending order, include such candidates as the Staffordshire Bull Terrier, causing a reported $302. (£178.) worth of damage over the dog's lifetime, followed by the West Highland White Terrier, Yorkshire Terrier, Spaniel, Whippet, Shih Tzu, Labrador, Jack Russell, Rottweiler and Sheepdog.

With all the cross breeding and creation of hybrid, designer canines these days, there are some very interesting studies being carried out, such as this one, that will help us humans better understand our favorite companions and what we may be letting ourselves in for.

NOTE: the more popular a particular breed may be, and the more positive traits a particular breed may enjoy will also make the cost of initially purchasing a puppy from a breeder more costly.

# Chapter 12: Coat Colors and Types

The Australian Labradoodle will tend toward having a non-shedding, softer, curly or wavy coat that will be more easily tolerated by human allergy sufferers.

What type of coat an Australian Labradoodle puppy will have is usually obvious around the age of 5 or 6 weeks.

Australian Labradoodle coat colors come in a wide variety, depending on the coat color of the parents and which parent's genes are more dominant.

When choosing an Australian Labradoodle as your companion, there are many coat color combinations possible, including:

- Apricot (also called gold, may fade in time)
- Black (no other color in the coat and nose also black)
- Blue (dark to medium smoky blue)
- Caramel (a rich gold)
- Cream (sometimes with apricot or gold tinting)
- Chocolate (dark and rich, born almost black)
- Multi-patterned (containing more than two colors)
- Red (can fade as the dog grows older)
- White (sometimes called chalk)
- Parchment (creamy chocolate)
- Parti (black and white)
- Phantom (solid base color, markings of a second color)

The ears of an Australian Labradoodle will be long and floppy, or pendant.

Unless the coat on the Australian Labradoodle tends more to the Labrador hair, it will generally be quite high maintenance, requiring brushing every few days to keep mats to a minimum and regular clipping several times a year.

## 1. Puppy Coats

The Australian Labradoodle puppy is not born with the fluffy or curly coat and will usually be soft and flat coated. The coat will start to thicken, curl and mat at approximately six months and this is when you will need to start a serious grooming regimen.

By the time the Australian Labradoodle puppy is twelve to fifteen months old, they will have completely grown in their adult coat.

The coat of the Australian Labradoodle may be more soft and wavy, or soft and curly, like their Poodle parent, can take on more of the straight, coarse texture of the Labrador Retriever, or can be a combination of the two parents.

The Australian Labradoodle hybrid coat can be a variety of colors including all the colors of a Labrador Retriever as well as all of the colors of the Poodle and every combination of the two.

## 2. Adult Coats

The Australian Labradoodle adult coat will begin to grow in at approximately 6 to 12 months of age. The entire process and complete change over to the adult coat will usually take 3 or 4 months or longer to fully complete.

During this time of coat change over, it will be very important to thoroughly brush or rake out your young dog's coat every day to help remove dead hair, mats and tangles, while the new coat grows in.

## 3. Coat Types

Within the Australian Labradoodle breed there are three distinctly different coat types, including the hair coat, which is a flat coat, the fleece coat, which has a soft wave or curl and a soft feel, and the wool or tightly curled coat that has a dense feel.

**Hair Coat**: the hair coat will be of a straighter, coarser texture, will shed and may not be a good choice for allergy sufferers. This type of coat will not require clipping.

**Fleece Coat**: will be an allergy free wavy coat that will usually have a soft, spiraling curl and will feel silky and soft to the touch. This type of coat requires regular grooming in order to ensure reduce matting. There will be little to no shedding and no body odor and this type of coat will require trimming several times a year.

**Wool Coat:** this is a tightly curled coat that will be allergy free and have the appearance of spiraling wool while feeling soft and dense, and there will be no body odor. This type of coat will require more regular clipping.

Regular grooming will also be essential for keeping their coat in good shape and condition.

## 4. Defining Features

The most distinctive features of the Australian Labradoodle are their soft wavy or curly, non-shedding coat, long ears and their joyful, friendly temperaments.

# Chapter 13: Grooming

You will want to get your Australian Labradoodle puppy used to the routine of grooming early on, so that they will not be traumatized for the rest of their life, every time grooming is necessary.

The Australian Labradoodle has a high maintenance type of coat. Not taking the time to regularly involve your puppy in grooming sessions could lead to serious, unwanted behavior that may include trauma to your dog, not to mention stress or injury to yourself in the form of biting and scratching, that could result in a lifetime of unhappy grooming sessions.

When you neglect regular, daily or at least a weekly at home grooming session with your puppy or dog to remove dead hair and check toenails, this will not only cost you and your canine companion, in terms of possible trauma it may also cost you in veterinarian fees should you not be aware of a problem that could have been discovered early on during regular grooming sessions.

An effective home regimen will depend on the length of your Australian Labradoodle's coat, and should include not just surface brushing, but also getting to all those sensitive areas easily missed around the ears and collar area, the armpit area, and the back end and tail.

Do not allow yourself to get caught in the *"my dog doesn't like it"* trap, which is an excuse many owners will use to avoid regular grooming sessions.

When you allow your dog to dictate whether they will permit a grooming session, you are setting a dangerous precedent that could lead to a lifetime of trauma for both you and your dog.

When humans neglect daily grooming routines, many dogs develop a heightened sensitivity, especially with regard to having their legs and feet held, their ears inspected, or their nails clipped, and will do anything they can to avoid the process when you need to groom them.

Make a pact with yourself right from the first day you bring your Australian Labradoodle puppy home, never to neglect a regular grooming routine and not to avoid sensitive areas, such as regular brushing, trimming toenails or brushing teeth, just because your dog may not particularly *"like"* it.

Remember that a few minutes of regular grooming sessions each day with your Australian Labradoodle is also wonderful opportunity for closely bonding.

## 1. Bath Time

Step One: before you get your Australian Labradoodle anywhere near the water, it's important to make sure that you brush out any debris, dead hair, mats or tangles from their coat before you begin the bathing process.

As well, removing any debris or mats from your dog's coat beforehand will make the entire process easier on both you, your dog, and your drains, which will become clogged with dead hair if you don't remove it beforehand.

Step Two: if your Australian Labradoodle has a longer coat, the process will be much easier if you first spray the coat with a light mist of leave-in conditioner before brushing. This will also help to protect the hair strands against breakage.

Step Three: whether you're bathing your Australian Labradoodle in your laundry tub, bathtub or sink, you will always want to first lay down a rubber bath mat to provide a more secure footing for your dog and to prevent your tub or sink from being scratched.

Step Four: have everything you need for the bath (shampoo, conditioner, sponge, towels) right next to the sink or tub, so you don't have to go searching once your dog is already in the water.

**TIP**: place cotton balls in your Australian Labradoodle's ear canals to prevent accidental splashes from entering the ear canal that could later cause an ear infection.

Step Five: fill the tub or sink with four to six inches of lukewarm water (not too hot as dogs are more sensitive to hot water than us humans) and put your Australian Labradoodle in the water. Completely wet your dog's coat right down to the skin by using a detachable showerhead. If you don't have a spray attachment, a cup or pitcher will work just as well.

**TIP**: no dog likes to have water poured over its head and into its eyes, so use a wet sponge or wash cloth to wet the head area.

Step Six: apply shampoo as indicated on the bottle instructions by beginning at the head and working your way down the back. Be careful not to get shampoo in the eyes, nose, mouth or ears. Comb the shampoo lather through your dog's hair with your fingers, making sure you don't miss the areas under the legs and tail.

Step Seven: after allowing the shampoo to remain in your dog's coat for a couple of minutes, thoroughly rinse the Australian Labradoodle's coat, right down to the skin with clean, lukewarm water using the spray attachment, cup or pitcher. Comb through your dog's coat with your fingers to make sure all shampoo residue has been completely rinsed away.

**TIP**: any shampoo remaining in a dog's coat will lead to irritation and itching. Once you've rinsed, take the time to rinse again, especially in the armpits and underneath the tail area.

Use your hands to gently squeeze all excess water from your dog's coat.

Step Eight: apply conditioner as indicated on the bottle instructions and work the conditioner throughout your Australian Labradoodle's coat. Leave the conditioner in your dog's coat for two minutes and then thoroughly rinse again with warm water, unless the conditioner you are using is a *"leave-in"*, no-rinse formula.

**NOTE**: The best conditioner for a Australian Labradoodle will contain mink oil, which adds a gloss to deepen and enrich the natural color of the coat.

It is also a good idea to choose a brand of conditioner that contains sunscreen to help protect from ultraviolet radiation when your dog is outside on sunny days, and to protect their skin when they are clipped short.

Applying a good conditioner containing protein to your Australian Labradoodle's coat after bathing will help to rebuild, restructure and protect the coat by bonding to the shaft of each individual hair.

Pull the plug on your sink or tub and let the water drain away as you use your hands to squeeze excess water from your Australian Labradoodle's legs and feet.

Step Nine: immediately out of the water, wrap your Australian Labradoodle in dry towels so they don't get cold and use the towels to gently squeeze out extra water before you allow them to shake and spray water everywhere.

If your dog has longer hair, do not rub their coat with the towels, as this will create tangles and breakage in the longer hair.

Dry your Australian Labradoodle right away with your hand held hairdryer and be careful not to let the hot air get too close to their skin.

**TIP**: if your Australian Labradoodle's hair is longer, blow the hair in the direction of growth to help prevent breakage and if the hair is short, you can use your hand or a soft brush or comb to lift and fluff the coat to help it dry more quickly.

**TIP**: place your hand between the hairdryer and your Australian Labradoodle's hair so that they will never get a direct blast of hot air and never blow air directly into their face or ears.

Don't forget to remove the cotton balls from their ears.

## 2. Ear Care

There are many ear cleaning creams, drops, oils, rinses, solutions and wipes formulated for cleaning your dog's ears that you can purchase from your local pet store or veterinarian's office.

Or you may prefer to use a home remedy that will just as efficiently clean your Australian Labradoodle's ears, such as Witch Hazel or a 50:50 mixture of hydrogen peroxide and purified water.

**TIP**: if you are going to make your own ear cleaning solution, find a bottle with a nozzle, measure your solution, properly diluted and mixed into the bottle, and use your preparation to saturate a cotton makeup remove pad to wipe out the visible part of your dog's ears. Always make sure the ears are totally dried after cleaning.

## 3. Eye Care

Every dog should have their eyes regularly wiped with a warm, damp cloth to remove build up of daily secretions in the corners of the eyes that can be unattractive and uncomfortable for the dog as the hair becomes glued together.

If this build up is not removed every day, it can quickly become a cause of bacterial yeast growth that can lead to eye infections.

When you take a moment every day to gently wipe your dog's eyes with a warm, moist cloth, you will help to keep your dog's eyes comfortable and infection free.

## 4. Nail Care

Allowing your Australian Labradoodle to have long, untrimmed nails can result in various health hazards including infections or an irregular and uncomfortable gait that can result in damage to their skeleton.

Although most dogs do not particularly enjoy the process of having their nails trimmed, and most humans find the exercise to be a little scary, regular nail trimming is a very important grooming practice that should never be overlooked.

When you get them used to having their nails trimmed at a young age, they will quietly tolerate the process for the rest of their life.

In order to keep your adult Australian Labradoodle's toenails in good condition and the proper length, you will need to purchase a plier type nail trimmer at a pet store and learn how to correctly use it.

Generally speaking, if you can hear your dog's nails clacking or scratching on the floor or road surface when they walk, their nails are too long, and if you continue to allow your dog's nails to be too long, the nail quick will grow longer into the nail, which will make it more difficult to keep them trimmed to the correct length.

**NOTE**: when your Australian Labradoodle is a small puppy, it will be best to trim their nails with a pair of nail scissors, which you can purchase at any pet store, that are smaller and easier to use on puppy nails. All you need to do is snip off the curved tip of each nail.

Further, if you want your dog's nails to be smooth, without the sharp edges clipping alone can create, you will also want to invest in a toenail file or a special, slow speed, rotary Dremel™ trimmer, equipped with a sanding disk, which is designed especially for dog nails.

Some dogs will prefer the rotary trimmer to the squeezing sensation of the nail clipper and when you keep your dog's nails regularly trimmed, the Dremel™ may be the only tool you will ever need.

**NOTE**: never use a regular Dremel™ tool on a dog's toenails as it will be too high speed and will burn your dog's toenails. Only use a slow speed Dremel™, Model 7300-PT Pet Nail Grooming Tool.

## 5. Dental Care

As a conscientious Australian Labradoodle guardian you will need to regularly care for your dog's teeth throughout their entire life.

### a) Retained Primary Teeth

Often times a young dog will not naturally lose their puppy or baby teeth, especially those with small jaws, like the Australian Labradoodle, without intervention from a licensed veterinarian. Therefore, keep a close watch on your puppy's teeth around the age of 6 or 7 months of age to make certain that the baby teeth have fallen out and that the adult teeth have space to grow in.

If your Australian Labradoodle puppy has not naturally lost all their baby teeth, any remaining teeth will need to be pulled, in order to allow room for the adult teeth to properly grow in, and the best time to do this will be at the same time they visit the veterinarian's office to be spayed or neutered.

NOTE: a smaller Australian Labradoodle will have a smaller jaw, which can result in more problems with teeth overcrowding.

An overcrowded mouth can cause teeth to grow unevenly or crooked and food and plaque to more easily build up, which will eventually result in bacterial growth on the surface of the teeth, causing bad breath, gum and dental disease.

**b) Periodontal Disease**

Please be aware that 80% of three-year-old dogs suffer from periodontal disease and bad breath because their guardians do not look after their dog's teeth.

What makes this shocking statistic even worse is that with simple, daily care, it is possible to entirely prevent canine gum disease and bad breath.

The pain associated with periodontal disease will make your dog's life miserable, as it will be painful for them to eat and the associated bacteria can infect many parts of the dog's body, including the heart, kidney, liver and brain, all of which they will have to suffer in silence.

If your Australian Labradoodle has bad breath, this could be the first sign of an unhealthy mouth and gum disease caused by plaque build-up on the teeth. As well, if your Australian Labradoodle is drooling excessively, this may be a symptom secondary to dental disease. Your dog may be experiencing pain or the salivary glands may be reacting to inflammation from excessive bacteria in the mouth.

If you notice your Australian Labradoodle drooling, you will want to have them professionally examined at your veterinarian's office.

**c) Teeth Brushing**

Slowly introduce your Australian Labradoodle to teeth brushing early on in their young life so that they will not fear it.

Begin with a finger cap toothbrush when they are young puppies, and then move to a soft bristled toothbrush, or even an electric brush, as all you have to do is hold it against the teeth while the brush does all the work. Sometimes with a manual brush, you may brush too hard and cause the gums to bleed.

Never use human toothpaste or mouthwash on your dog's teeth because dogs cannot spit and human toothpaste that contains toxic fluoride will be swallowed. There are many flavored dog toothpastes available at the pet store or veterinarian's office.

Also, it's a good idea to get your dog used to the idea of occasionally having their teeth scraped or scaled, especially the back molars which tend to build up plaque. Be very careful if you are doing this yourself because the tools are sharp.

TIP: if you need help keeping your dog's mouth open while you do a quick brush or scrape, get yourself a piece of hard material (rubber or leather) that they can bite down on, so that they cannot fully close their mouth while you work on their teeth.

When your Australian Labradoodle is a young puppy, take the time to get them used to having their mouth handled and your fingers rubbing their teeth and gums.

Next, buy some canine toothpaste at your local pet store specially flavored to appeal to dogs and apply this to your dog's teeth with your finger.

Then slowly introduce the manual or electric toothbrush to your Australian Labradoodle. When you go slowly, they will get used to the buzzing and vibrating of the electric brush, which will do a superior job of cleaning their teeth.

First, let them see the electric brush, then let them hear it buzzing, and before you put it in their mouth, let them feel the buzzing sensation on their body, while you move it slowly toward their head and muzzle.

When your Australian Labradoodle will allow you to touch their muzzle while the brush is turned on, the next step is to lift their lip and quickly brush a couple of teeth at a time until they get used to having them all brushed at the same time.
Always happily praise them for allowing you to brush their teeth, especially when they are first getting used to the idea.

**TIP**: another simple home solution for helping to keep your dog's breath fresh and their teeth white is Bicarbonate of Soda (baking soda). Simply sprinkle some into a dish and dip your finger or toothbrush first in water and then into the Bicarbonate of Soda. Then use this to clean your dog's teeth and massage their gums. Some dogs seem to object less to this procedure when you use your finger.

Whether you let the electric toothbrush do the work for you, or you are using your finger or a manual toothbrush, make certain that you brush in a circular motion and when using a brush, angle the bristles so that they extend underneath the gums to help prevent plaque buildup, gum disease and loose teeth.

## d) Teeth Scaling

Use of a tooth scraper or scaling tool once or twice a month can help to remove plaque buildup. Most accumulation will be found on the outside of the teeth and on the back molars, near the gum line.

Go slowly and carefully because these tools are sharp and only do this when your dog is calm and relaxed, a little bit at a time.

## e) Healthy Teeth Tips

Despite what most dog owners might put up with as normal, it is not normal for your dog to have smelly dog breath or canine halitosis.

Bad breath is the first sign of an unhealthy mouth, which could involve gum disease or tooth decay.

The following tips will help keep your Australian Labradoodle's mouth and teeth healthy:

- Keep your dog's teeth sparkling white and their breath fresh by using old-fashioned hydrogen peroxide as your doggy toothpaste. Hydrogen peroxide is what's in the human whitening toothpaste. There will be such a small amount on the brush that it will not harm your dog, and will kill any bacteria in your dog's mouth.

- Many canine toothpastes are formulated with active enzymes to help keep tartar build-up at bay.

- Help prevent tooth plaque and doggy halitosis by feeding your dog natural, hard bones at least once a month, which will also help to remove tartar while polishing and keeping their teeth white.

- Feed large bones so there is no danger of swallowing, and do NOT boil the bones first because this makes the bone soft (which defeats the purpose of removing plaque), and boiling could cause bones to splinter into smaller pieces that could create a choking or puncturing hazard for your dog.

- Smaller dogs, such as the Australian Labradoodle, tend to be more vulnerable to teeth and gum problems, therefore, you really need to be brushing their teeth every single day.

- Feed a daily dental chew or hard biscuit to help to remove tartar while exercising jaws and massaging gums. Some dental chews contain natural breath freshening cinnamon, cloves or chlorophyll.

- Coconut oil also helps to prevent smelly dog breath while giving your dog's digestive, immune and metabolic functions a boost at the same time. Dogs love the taste, so add ¼ teaspoon to your Australian Labradoodle's dinner and their breath will soon be much sweeter.

Keep your Australian Labradoodle's mouth comfortable and healthy by getting into the habit of brushing their teeth every night before bedtime.

## 6. Skin Care

Keeping your Australian Labradoodle's coat clean by regularly bathing with canine shampoo and conditioner and free from mats, debris and parasites, as well as providing plenty of clean water and feeding them a high quality diet free from allergy-causing ingredients will go a long way toward keeping their skin healthy and itch-free and their coat shiny and healthy looking.

Between bath times, there are many moist doggy wipes on the market that are especially formulated with the correct pH balance to help keep your dog clean and their skin healthy. Consider getting into the habit of wiping down your dog with one of these moist towels every night before bed.

## 7. Pest Control

### a) Fleas

Every dog usually picks up a flea or two sometime in their

lifetime, so you should be prepared for this inevitability by ensuring that you have a good flea shampoo on hand as well as a flea comb.

If you notice your dog biting, scratching or chewing at his or herself, the chances that they have picked up a flea or two is quite high, so it's time for a flea bath.

### b) Ticks

If your dog goes roaming freely through wooded and bushy areas with large trees, they may also pick up the occasional tick.

Always carefully check through your dog's coat and ears after they have been romping through the woods, and make sure that you also have a solution on hand that will kill a tick or the proper tool that can easily and safely twist any size of tick out of a dog's skin.

A very effective product, which is 100% safe for humans and animals, that will kill ticks on contact, is a natural pest control product made by CedarCide called *"Best Yet Organic Bug Spray"*.

As well, ticks can be quickly and easily removed with a simple to use *"Tick Twister"*.

## 8. Brushing and Combing

An often over looked task, that is a necessary part of maintaining the health of an Australian Labradoodle, is daily brushing and combing.

As well, taking time to brush and comb your Australian Labradoodle's coat will also give you an opportunity to bond with your dog, while identifying any problems (such as fatty lumps or bumps and matted hair) early on, before they may become more serious.

Make sure that your grooming sessions are as pleasant as possible by choosing the right tools for an Australian Labradoodle and their type and length of coat.

You will need minimal brushes and combs to keep your Australian Labradoodle's coat in good condition, including a slicker brush and a bristle brush.

As well as one or two brushes, and a comb, it's always a good idea to need to invest in a mat splitter, a rake and a flea comb.

## 9. Equipment Required

A slicker brush has short, thin, wire bristles arranged closely together and anchored to a flat, often rectangular, surface that's attached to a handle.

A slicker brush is an ideal grooming tool for helping to remove mats and tangles from an Australian Labradoodle who has a longer coat. Slicker brushes are often used as a finishing brush after brushing with the bristle brush to smooth the dog's coat and create a shiny finish.

A bristle brush can be used to help remove debris and dead hair from the coat and also to help distribute natural oils to keep the coat looking healthy and shiny.

A metal comb can also be used for grooming longer haired Australian Labradoodle. Most metal combs have a combination of widely spaced and narrow spaced teeth and are designed so that if you run into a tangle, you can switch to the wider spaced teeth while you work it out, without pulling and irritating your dog.

**NOTE**: Some combs have rotating teeth, which makes the process of removing tangles from your Australian Labradoodle's coat much easier on them without the pain of pulling and snagging.

Mat splitters are, as the name suggests, designed to split apart matted fur or hair so that you can then comb out the areas. Mats can quickly occur underneath the belly, in the armpits and tail area or around the neck.

A rake (which looks like a tiny rake) is very helpful for removing dead hair when your puppy is changing from their puppy coat to the new adult coat.

Flea combs, as the name suggests, are designed for the specific purpose of removing fleas from a dog's coat.

A flea comb is usually small in size for maneuvering in tight spaces, and may be made of plastic or metal with the teeth of the comb placed very close together to trap hiding fleas.

A Tick Twister, is a simple device for painlessly, easily and quickly removing ticks that have imbedded themselves in your dog's skin.

Nail clippers or scissors (and/or a slow speed pet Dremel™) will be tools you need to use every couple of weeks or more, depending on how quickly your dog's nails grow and what types of surfaces they may be walking on.

## 10. Products

### a) Shampoos

NEVER make the mistake of using human shampoo or conditioner for bathing your Australian Labradoodle because dogs have a different pH balance than humans.

For example, shampoo for humans has a pH balance of 5.5, whereas shampoo formulated for our canine companions has an almost neutral pH balance of 7.5.

Any shampoo with a lower pH balance will be harmful to your dog because it will be too harshly acidic for their coat and skin, which can create skin problems.

Always purchase a shampoo for your dog that is specially formulated to be gentle and moisturizing on your Australian Labradoodle's coat and skin, that will not strip the natural oils, and which will nourish your dog's coat to give it a healthy shine.

As a general rule, always read the instructions provided on the shampoo bottle, and avoid shampoos containing insecticides or harsh chemicals.

**TIP**: if your dog is suffering from an infestation of fleas, you may want to bathe them with shampoo containing pyrethrum (a botanical extract found in small, white daisies) or a shampoo containing citrus or tea tree oil, or bath and spray them with the very effective CedarCide products which can also be used to spray down their bedding and any carpets in the home.

**b) Conditioners**

While many of us humans use a conditioner after we shampoo our own hair, a large number of canine guardians forget to use a conditioner on our own dog's coat after bathing.

Even if the bathing process is one that you wish to complete as quickly as possible, you will want to reconsider this little oversight because, just as conditioning our human hair improves its condition, the same is true for our dog's coat.

Conditioning your Australian Labradoodle's coat will not only make it look and feel better, conditioning will also add additional benefits, including:

- Preventing the escape of natural oils and moisture;
- Keeping the coat cleaner for a longer period of time;

- Repairing a coat that has become damaged or dry;
- Restoring a soft, silky feel;
- Helping the coat dry more quickly;
- Protection from the heat of the dryer and breakage of longer coats during toweling, combing or brushing;

Spend the extra two minutes to condition your Australian Labradoodle's coat after bathing. The benefits of doing so will be appreciated by both yourself and your dog that will have overall healthy skin and a coat with a natural shine.

**c) De-tanglers**

There are many de-tangling products you can purchase which will make the job of combing a longer coat much easier on both you and your Australian Labradoodle.

De-tangling products work by making the hair slippery, and while some de-tanglers work well when used full strength, you may prefer a lighter, spray-in product.

As well, there are silicone products and grooming powders, or you can even use cornstarch to effectively lubricate the hair to help with removing mats and tangles before bathing.

**d) Styptic Powder**

You will always want to avoid causing any pain when trimming your Australian Labradoodle's toenails, because you don't want to destroy their trust in you regularly performing this necessary task.

However, accidents do happen, therefore if you accidentally cut into the vein in the toenail, know that you will cause your dog pain, and that the toenail will bleed.

Therefore, it is always a good idea to keep some styptic powder (often called *"Kwik Stop")* in your grooming kit. Dip a moistened finger into the powder and apply it to the end of the bleeding nail.

The quickest way to stop a nail from bleeding is to immediately apply styptic powder and firm pressure for a few seconds.

**TIP**: if you do not have styptic powder available, there are several home remedies that can help stop the bleeding, including a mixture of baking soda and cornstarch, or simply cornstarch alone. Also, a cold, wet teabag or rubbing with scent-free soap can also be effective. These home remedies will not be as instantly effective as styptic powder.

**e) Ear Powders**

Ear powders, which can be purchased at any pet store, are designed to help keep your dog's ears dry while at the same time inhibiting the growth of bacteria that can lead to infections. Ear powders are also used when removing excess hair growth from inside a dog's ear canal as the powder makes it easier to grip the hair.

**f) Ear Cleaning Solutions**

Your local pet store will offer a wide variety of ear cleaning creams, drops, oils, rinses or wipes specially formulated for cleaning your dog's ears.

As well, there are also many home remedies that will just as efficiently clean your dog's ears without the high price tag.

**NOTE**: because a dog's ears are a very sensitive area, always read the labels before purchasing products and avoid any solutions that list alcohol as the main ingredient.

**g) Home Ear Cleaning Solutions**

The following are three effective home solutions that will efficiently clean your dog's ears:

Witch Hazel is a natural anti-inflammatory that works well to cleanse and protect against infection while encouraging faster healing of minor skin traumas.

A 50:50 solution of Organic Apple Cider Vinegar and Purified Water has been used as an external folk medicine for decades. This mixture is a gentle and effective solution that kills germs while naturally healing.

A 50:50 solution of Hydrogen Peroxide and Purified Water is useful for cleansing wounds and dissolving earwax.

Whatever product you decide to use for cleaning your dog's ears, always be careful about what you put into your dog's ears and thoroughly dry them after cleaning.

**h) Canine Toothpastes**

When it comes time to brush a dog's teeth, this is where many guardians fail miserably, often using the excuse that *"my dog doesn't like it"*.

Whether they like it or otherwise is not the issue, because in order to keep your Australian Labradoodle healthy, they must have healthy teeth and the only way to ensure this, is to brush their teeth every day.

The many canine toothpastes on the market are usually flavored with beef or chicken in an attempt to appeal to the dog's taste buds, while others may be infused with mint or some other breath freshening ingredient in an attempt to appeal to humans by improving the dog's breath.

Honestly, your dog is not going to be begging for you to brush his or her teeth no matter how tasty the paste might be, therefore, effectiveness, in the shortest period of time, will be more of a deciding factor than whether or not your dog prefers the taste of the toothpaste.

Some dog toothpastes contain baking soda, which is the same mild abrasive found in many human pastes, and is designed to gently scrub the teeth. However, just how much time you will have to spend scrubbing your dog's teeth, before they've had enough, may be too minimal to make these pastes very effective.

Other types of canine toothpastes are formulated with enzymes that are designed to work chemically by breaking down tartar or plaque in the dog's mouth. These pastes do not need to be washed off your dog's teeth and are safe for them to swallow. Whether or not they remain on the dog's teeth long enough to do any good might be debatable.

**TIP**: old-fashioned hydrogen peroxide cleans while killing germs and keeping teeth white. Just dip your dog's toothbrush in a capful of hydrogen peroxide, shake off the excess, and brush their teeth. There will be such a small amount in your dog's mouth that you don't need to worry about them swallowing it.

### i) Paw Creams

Depending upon the types of surfaces our canine counterparts usually walk on, they may suffer from cracked or rough pads. You can restore resiliency and keep your Australian Labradoodle's paws in healthy condition by regularly applying a cream or lotion to protect their paw pads.

TIP: a good time to do this is just after you have clipped their nails.

**NOTE**: if you live in a hot climate, be aware that sidewalks, road surfaces and sandy beaches can get extremely hot for your dog's feet. As well, a smaller sized Australian Labradoodle is that much closer to the hot surface, which means that on a hot day, they will be feeling the effects of being heated from both sides. If you live in a very hot climate, choose to walk them during the cooler hours of the day, walk them on grassy areas only, or carry them.

### j) Organic Pest Control

CedarCide is a company that makes 100% safe, organic products to control biting bugs on your fur friends without worrying about harmful chemicals that are not good for you, your children or your canine companions.

Simply spray it on, and bugs of any sort that come into contact with the solution will be dead, while your dog's coat will be shiny and fresh smelling, like the inside of a cedar chest.

## 11. Professional Grooming

If you decide that you are not interesting in buying all the equipment (electric clippers, blades, scissors, nail clippers, combs, brushes, table, etc.) or enrolling yourself in a $4,000 (£2,388) course to learn how to professionally groom your Australian Labradoodle yourself, you will want to locate a trusted professional service to do this for you.

The best way to find a groomer is to ask others who they use and whether they are happy with the results.

If you have decided to keep your Australian Labradoodle clipped short, you will need to take them for a full grooming session approximately every 6 to 8 weeks.

An average price for professionally grooming a Australian Labradoodle will usually start around $60 (£40) and could be considerably more depending upon the size of the dog and whether the salon is also bathing and trimming nails.

# Chapter 14: Socializing

Most Australian Labradoodles are naturally friendly, happy and social dogs, however, they will still need to be exposed to different people, places and unusual sights and sounds when they are puppies.

Any dog that is not regularly socialized may become shy or suspicious of unfamiliar or unusual people or circumstances, which could lead to nervous or fearful behavior.

## 1. With Other Dogs and Pets

Generally speaking, the majority of an adult dog's habits and behavioral traits will be formed between the ages of birth and one year of age.

This is why it will be very important to introduce your Australian Labradoodle puppy to a wide variety of locations, sights, sounds, smells and situations during this formative period in their young life.

Your Australian Labradoodle puppy will learn how to behave, in all these various circumstances, by following your lead, feeling your energy and watching how you react in every situation.

For instance, never accidentally reward your Australian Labradoodle puppy or dog for displaying nervousness, fear or growling at another dog or person by picking them up.

Picking up an Australian Labradoodle puppy or dog at this time, when they are displaying unbalanced energy, actually turns out to be a reward for them, and you will be teaching them to continue with this type of behavior.

As well, picking up a puppy places them in a top dog position, where they have the higher ground and literally (because they are higher up) become more dominant than the person or dog they may have just growled at.

The correct action to take in such a situation is to gently correct your Australian Labradoodle puppy, with a firm, yet calm energy by distracting them with a “no”, or a quick sideways snap of the leash to get their attention back on you, so that they learn to let you deal with the situation on their behalf.

If you allow a fearful, nervous or shy puppy deal with situations that unnerve them without your direction, they may learn to react with fear or aggression to unfamiliar circumstances and you will have created a problem that could escalate into something more serious as they grow older.

The same is true of situations where a young puppy may feel the need to protect itself from a larger or older dog that may come charging in for a sniff.

It is the guardian’s responsibility to protect the puppy so that they do not feel that they must react with fear or aggression in order to protect themselves.

Once your Australian Labradoodle puppy has received all their vaccinations, you can take them out to public dog parks and various locations where many dogs and people are found.

Before allowing them to interact with other dogs or puppies, take them for a disciplined walk on leash so that they will be a little tired and less likely to immediately pounce excitedly on all other dogs.

Keep your puppy on leash and close beside you, because most young puppies are a bundle of out of control energy, and you need to protect them while teaching them how far they can go before they may get themselves into trouble with adult dogs that might not appreciate their excited playfulness.

Remember that they may not have experienced the company of other dogs since you brought them home, and now that they have completed their course of vaccinations, they will understandably be excited and perhaps a little hesitant about seeing dogs again.

Keep a close watch on your Australian Labradoodle puppy to make sure they are not being overwhelmed by too many other dogs, or getting overly excited and stressed or nervous, because it is your job to protect your puppy.

If your puppy shows any signs of aggression or domination toward another puppy, dog or person, you must immediately step in and calmly discipline them, otherwise by doing nothing, you will be agreeing with their behavior and will be allowing them to get into situations that could become serious behavioral issues as they grow in age and size.

No matter the age or size of your Australian Labradoodle puppy, allowing them to display aggression or domination over another dog or person is never a laughing matter and this type of behavior must be immediately curtailed.

## 2. With Other People

Take your puppy everywhere with you and introduce them to many different people of all ages, sizes and ethnicities.

This will be easy to do, because most people will automatically be drawn to you when they see you have a puppy because few humans can resist a puppy, especially one as cute as an Australian Labradoodle.

Most humans will want to interact with your puppy and if they ask to hold your puppy, this is a good opportunity to socialize your puppy and show them that humans are friendly.

Do not let others (especially young children) play roughly with your puppy or squeal at them in a high-pitched voices because this can be very frightening for a sensitive young puppy, such as the Australian Labradoodle.

As well, you do not want to teach your puppy that humans are a source of crazy, excited energy.

Be especially careful when introducing your puppy to young children who may accidentally hurt your puppy, because you don't want your dog to become fearful of children as this could lead to aggression issues later on in life.

Explain to children that your Australian Labradoodle puppy is very young and that they must be calm and gentle when playing or interacting in any way.

## 3. Within Different Environments

It can be a big mistake not to take the time to introduce your Australian Labradoodle puppy to a wide variety of different environments because when they are not comfortable with different sights and sounds, this could cause them possible trauma later in their adult life.

Be creative and take your puppy everywhere you can imagine when they are young so that no matter where they travel, whether strolling along a noisy city sidewalk or beside a peaceful shoreline, they will be equally comfortable.

Do not make the mistake of only taking your Australian Labradoodle puppy into areas where you live and will always travel because they need to also be comfortable visiting areas you might not often visit, such as noisy construction sites, airports or a shopping area across town.

Your puppy needs to see all sorts of sights, sounds and situations so that they will not become fearful should they need to travel with you to any of these areas.

Your Australian Labradoodle puppy will take their cues from you, which means that when you are calm and in control of every situation, they will learn to be the same because they will trust your lead.

For instance, put your puppy in their Sherpa bag and take them to the airport where they can watch people and hear planes landing and taking off.

Take them to a local park where they can see a baseball game, or for a stroll beside a schoolyard at recess time when noisy children are out playing, or take them to the local zoo or farm and let them get a close up look at horses, pigs and ducks.

## 4. Loud Noises

Many dogs can show extreme fear of loud noises, such as fireworks or thunderstorms.

If you take the time to desensitize your Australian Labradoodle to these types of noises when they are very young, it will be much easier on them during stormy weather or holidays such as Halloween or New Year's when fireworks are often a part of the festivities.

You can purchase CD's that are a collection of unusual sounds, such as vacuums or hoovers, airplanes, people clapping hands, screaming children, and more, that you can play while working in your kitchen or relaxing in your living room or lounge.

When you play these sounds and pretend that everything is normal, the next time your puppy or dog hears these types of sounds elsewhere, they will not become upset or agitated because they have learned to ignore them.

Also make sure that you get your young puppy used to the sounds of thunder and fireworks at an early age because these types of shrieking, crashing, banging and popping sounds of fireworks or thunder as well as the high pitched beeping of household smoke and fire alarms can be so traumatic and unsettling for many dogs, that sometimes, no matter how much you try to calm your dog, or pretend that everything is fine, there is little you can do.

Some dogs literally lose their minds when they hear the loud popping or screeching noises of fireworks and alarms and start running or trying to hide and you cannot communicate with them at all.

Make sure that your dog cannot harm itself trying to escape from these types of noises, and if possible, calmly hold them until they begin to relax.

If your dog loses it's mind when it hears these types of noises, simply avoid taking them anywhere near fireworks and if at times when they might hear these noises going off outside, play your inside music or TV louder than you might normally, to help disguise the exterior noise of fireworks or thunder.

As well, some dogs will respond well to wearing a *"ThunderShirt"* which is specifically designed to alleviate anxiety or trauma associated with loud rumbling, popping or banging noises. The idea behind the design of the ThunderShirt is that the gentle pressure it creates is similar to a hug that, for some dogs, has a calming effect.

Do not underestimate the importance of taking the time to continually (not just when they are puppies) socialize and desensitize your puppy to all manner of sights, sounds, individuals and locations because to do so will be teaching them to be a calm and well balanced member of your family that will quietly follow you in every situation.

# Chapter 15: Training

## 1. Trainability

As the Australian Labradoodle is a mixture of many different very intelligent breeds, they will almost undoubtedly also be an intelligent, willing to please and easy to train dog.

When taught with positive reinforcement, they will be eager learners who will easily excel at anything you have the time and patience to teach, and the more the better for this dog.

No matter what you decide to teach your Australian Labradoodle, always train with patience and kindness and NEVER yell, hit or punish a dog during training, or at any time for that matter.

Using harsh, mean or loud training methods could frighten an Australian Labradoodle and cause them to shut down.

As well, any sort of harsh treatment will cause your friendly and sensitive Australian Labradoodle to lose trust and respect of you, and they could also learn to fear you, which is NOT the type of relationship you want to have with your dog.

All training sessions should be happy and fun filled with plenty of rewards and positive reinforcement, which will ensure that your Australian Labradoodle is an excellent student who looks forward to learning new commands and tricks. The Australian Labradoodle can be highly skillful in many different forms of advanced dog sports, including Agility, Dock Diving, Obedience, Field Trials, Freestyle Dance, Rally, and more.

## 2. Puppy Training Basics

Most humans believe that they need to take their young dog to puppy classes, and generally speaking, this is a good idea for any young Australian Labradoodle (after they have had all their vaccinations), because it will help to get them socialized.

Beyond puppy classes for socializations reasons, hiring a professional dog whisperer for personalized private sessions to train the humans may be far more valuable than training situations where there are multiple dogs and humans together in one class as this can be very distracting for everyone concerned.

### a) Three Most Important Words

"Come", "Sit" and "Stay" will be the three most important words you will ever teach your Australian Labradoodle puppy.

These three basic commands will ensure that your Australian Labradoodle remains safe in almost every circumstance.

For instance, when your puppy correctly learns the "Come" command, you can always quickly bring them back to your side if you should see danger be approaching.

When you teach your Australian Labradoodle puppy the "Sit" and "Stay" commands you will be further establishing your leadership role. A puppy that understands that their human guardian is their leader will be a safe and happy follower.

### b) Choosing a Discipline Sound

Choosing a *"discipline sound"* that will be the same for every human family member will make it much easier for your puppy to learn what they can or cannot do and will be very useful when warning your Australian Labradoodle puppy before they engage in unwanted behavior.

The best types of sounds are short and sharp so that you and your family members can quickly say them and so that the sound will immediately get the attention of your Australian Labradoodle puppy because you want to be able to easily interrupt them when they are about to make a mistake.

It doesn't really matter what the sound is, so long as everyone in the family is consistent.

A sound that is very effective for most puppies and dogs is a simple *"UH"* sound said sharply and with emphasis.

Most puppies and dogs respond immediately to this sound and if caught in the middle of doing something they are not supposed to be doing will quickly stop and give you their attention or back away from what they were doing.

## 3. Beginner Leash Lesson

Equipment: 4 or 6-foot leash, Martingale training collar.

The most important ongoing bonding exercise you will experience with your new Australian Labradoodle puppy is when you go out for your daily walks together.

Far, far too many people ignore this critical, multi-tasking time that is not only important for your puppy's exercise, it fulfills a multitude of their needs, including:

- Exercising their body
- Fulfilling their natural roaming urges
- Teaching them discipline, which engages their mind
- Learning to follow, trust and respect you
- Reinforcing that you are their leader

As soon as you bring your new puppy home you will want to teach them how to walk at your side while on leash without pulling.

Every time your puppy needs to go out to relieve his or herself, slip on their collar and snap on that leash.

At first your Australian Labradoodle puppy may struggle or fight against having a collar around their neck, because the sensation will be new to them. However, at the same time they will want to go with you, so exercise patience and encourage them to walk with you.

Be careful never to drag them, and if they pull backward and refuse to walk forward with you, simply stop for a moment, while keeping slight forward tension on the leash, until your Australian Labradoodle puppy gives up and moves forward. Immediately reward them with your happy praise, and if they have a favorite treat, this can be an added incentive when teaching them to walk on their leash.

Always walk your puppy on your left side with the leash slack so that they learn that walking with you is a relaxing experience. Keep the leash short enough so that they do not have enough slack to get in front of you.

If they begin to create tension in the leash by pulling forward or to the side, simply stop moving, get them back beside you, and start over.

Be patient and consistent with your puppy and very soon they will understand exactly where their walking position is and will walk easily beside you without any pulling or leash tension.

Remember that walking with a new puppy is an exciting experience for them as they will want to sniff everything and explore their new world, so give them lots of understanding and don't expect them to be perfect all the time.

When your Australian Labradoodle puppy is very young, and wanting to put everything in their mouths, walk them in a harness AND collar and leash, so that you can have a second leash attached to the harness.

All puppies want to put everything in their mouths, therefore, when they are wearing a collar and leash, AND a harness and leash, you will be able to easily lift them over cigarette butts or other garbage you may encounter while out walking.

Once they grow out of the habit of tasting all manner of garbage, you can dispense with the harness and second leash.

## 4. Surviving Adolescence

The adolescent period in a young Australian Labradoodle's life, between the ages of 6 and 12 months, is the transitional stage of both physical and psychological development when they are physically almost full grown in size, yet their minds are still developing and they are testing their boundaries and the limits that their human counterparts will endure.

This can be a dangerous time in a puppy's life because this is when they start to make decisions on their own which, if they do not receive the leadership they need from their human guardians, can lead to developing unwanted behaviors.

Learning how to make decisions on their own would be perfectly normal and desirable if your Australian Labradoodle puppy was living in the wild, amongst a pack of dogs, because learning to make decisions would be necessary for their survival.

However, when living within a human environment, your puppy must always adhere to human rules and it will be up to their human guardians to continue their vigilant, watchful guidance in order to make sure that they do.

Many humans are lulled into a false sense of security when their new Australian Labradoodle puppy reaches the age of approximately six months, because the puppy has been well socialized, they have been to puppy classes and long since been house trained.

The real truth is that the serious work is only now beginning and the humans and their new Australian Labradoodle puppy could be in for a time of testing that could seriously challenge the relationship and leave the humans wondering if they made the right decision to share their home with a dog.

If the human side of the relationship is not prepared for this transitional time in their young dog's life, their patience may be seriously tried, and the relationship of trust and respect that has been previously built can be damaged, and could take considerable time to repair.

While not all adolescent puppies will experience a noticeable adolescent period of craziness, because every puppy is different, most young dogs do commonly exhibit at least some of the usual adolescent behaviors, including reverting to previous puppy behaviors.

Some of these adolescent behaviors might include destructive chewing of objects they have previously shown no interest in, selective hearing or ignoring previously learned commands, displaying aggressive behavior, barking uncontrollably, jumping on everyone, barking at everything that moves, or reverting to relieving themselves in the house, even though they were house trained months ago.

Keeping your cool and recognizing these adolescent signs is the first step toward helping to make this transition period easier on your Australian Labradoodle puppy and all family members.

The first step to take that can help keep raging hormones at bay, is to spay or neuter your Australian Labradoodle puppy just prior to the onset of adolescence, at around four or five months of age.

While spaying or neutering a Australian Labradoodle puppy will not entirely eliminate the adolescent phase, it will certainly help and at the same time will spare your puppy the added strain of both the physical and emotional changes that occur during sexual maturity.

As well, some female puppies will become extremely aggressive toward other dogs during a heat, and non-neutered males may become territorially aggressive and pick fights with other males.

Once your Australian Labradoodle puppy has been spayed or neutered, you will want to become more active with your young dog, both mentally and physically by providing them with continued and more complex disciplined exercises.

This can be accomplished by enrolling your adolescent Australian Labradoodle in a dog whispering session or more advanced training class, which will help them to continue their socialization skills while also developing their brain.

Even though it may be more difficult to train during this period, having the assistance of a professional and continuing the experience of ongoing socialization amongst other dogs of a similar size can be invaluable, as this is the time when many young dogs begin to show signs of antisocial behavior with other dogs as well as unknown humans.

When your Australian Labradoodle is provided with sufficient daily exercise and continued socialization with unfamiliar dogs, people and places that provides interest and expands their mind, they will be able to transition through the adolescent stage of their life much more seamlessly.

## 5. Releasing Energy

The adolescent period in any puppy's life is a time of boundless energy. Excess energy will be even more apparent in an intelligent, high energy Australian Labradoodle puppy and you will need to find ways to safely allow them to release this energy every day.

Since most humans cannot walk nearly fast enough to accommodate the needs of an energetic puppy, you will first want to walk your Australian Labradoodle beside you on leash, and then find a safe place where they can run off leash, either chasing a ball, retrieving a Frisbee or playing and running in an enclosed area with other similar sized dogs where you can always supervise.

## 6. The Unruly Adolescent

If your Australian Labradoodle puppy happens to be especially unruly during their adolescent phase, you will need to simply limit their opportunities for making mistakes.

For instance, a puppy who is digging up the yard, or chewing up just about anything they can get their teeth on will need to be closely supervised so that you can direct their energy into less harmful pursuits.

It does absolutely no good to yell at your Australian Labradoodle puppy for engaging in behavior you are not happy with, and in fact, yelling or getting angry will only desensitize your young dog from listening to any of your commands.

Further, although you may eventually get the results you want, if you yell loud enough, your puppy will then be reacting out of fear, rather than respect, and this will be damaging to your relationship.

Displaying calm, yet assertive energy is the ONLY energy that works well to help your adolescent puppy understand what is required of them.

All other human emotions (frustration, anger, impatience, sadness, excitement) are "read" by puppies and dogs as being unstable, and not only will the smart and sensitive Australian Labradoodle not understand these emotions, they will not respect you for displaying these types of unstable energies.

An extremely rambunctious adolescent Australian Labradoodle may need to have their free run of the house curtailed so that they are confined to areas where you can easily supervise them.

Make sure they are within eyesight at all times, so that if they do find an opportunity to make a mistake, you can quickly show them what is permitted and what is not.

Adolescence may also be a time when you might have to insist that your young companion sleeps in their crate with the door closed whenever you cannot supervise, as well as at bedtime so they continue to understand that you have firm rules.

As well, keeping on top of house training is also a good idea during the adolescent period of your puppy's life because some adolescent puppies may become stubborn and forget that they are already house trained.

This means actually taking the time to be involved in the process by leashing up your pup and physically taking them outside whenever they need to relieve themselves.

Many times humans that have back yards tend not to be very involved in the housebreaking routine because they just open a door and let their dogs run free in the back yard.

Too many humans with convenient yards simply do not participate at all in the bathroom routine of their young dogs and thereby miss out on endless opportunities to reinforce who is the boss.

## 7. Rewarding Unwanted Behavior

Often humans make the mistake of accidentally rewarding unwanted behaviors.

It is very important to recognize that any attention paid to an overly excited, out of control, adolescent puppy, even negative attention, is likely going to be rewarding for your puppy.

Therefore, when you engage with an out of control Australian Labradoodle puppy, you end up actually rewarding them, which will encourage them to continue more of this unwanted behavior.

Be aware that chasing after a puppy when they have taken something they are not supposed to have, picking them up when they are barking or showing aggression, pushing them off when they jump on you or other people, or yelling when they refuse to come when called, are all forms of attention that can actually be rewarding for most puppies.

As your Australian Labradoodle's guardian, it will be your responsibility to provide calm and consistent structure for your puppy, which will include finding acceptable and safe ways to allow your puppy to vent their energy without being destructive or harmful to property, other dogs, humans, or the actual puppy.

Activities that create or encourage an overly excited Australian Labradoodle puppy, such as rough games of tug-o-war, wild games of chase through the living room, or overly aggressive or excited play sessions with another dog or puppy, should be immediately curtailed, so that your adolescent puppy learns how to control their energy and play quietly and appropriately without jumping on everyone or engaging in barking or mouthy behavior.

Further, if your adolescent Australian Labradoodle puppy displays excited energy simply from being petted by yourself, your family members or any visitors, you will need to teach yourself, your family and your friends to ignore your puppy until they calm down. Otherwise, you will be inadvertently teaching your Australian Labradoodle puppy that the touch of humans means excitement.

For instance, when you continue to engage with an overly excited puppy or dog, you are rewarding them for out of control behavior and literally teaching them that when they see humans, you want them to display excited energy.

Worse, once your puppy has learned that humans are a source of excitement, you will then have to work very long and hard to reverse this behavior.

Children are often a source of excitement that can cause an adolescent puppy to be extremely wound up.

Do not allow your children to engage with an adolescent Australian Labradoodle puppy unless you are there to supervise and teach the children appropriate and calm ways to interact with the puppy.

In order to keep everyone safe, it is very important that your Australian Labradoodle puppy learn at an early age that neither children nor adults are sources of excitement.

You can help develop the mind of an adolescent Australian Labradoodle and the minds of growing children at the same time by teaching children that your puppy needs structured walks and by showing them how to play fetch, search, hide and seek, or how to teach the Australian Labradoodle puppy simple tricks and obedience skills that will be fun and positive interaction for everyone.

## 8. Back to Basics

When your puppy is going through what could be a belligerent and trying adolescence, when it seems that they have forgotten everything they may have already previously learned, this is an especially good time to revisit the simple "Sit" command.
Now, in order to help re-establish your leadership role, you will want to ask your Australian Labradoodle puppy to sit at every opportunity.

The simple act of "sitting" will help to calm an excited mind and will get your puppy's focus back on you.

## 9. Sit and More Sit

Every time you take your Australian Labradoodle out for a walk, which is often a cause of excitement, get into the habit of asking them to sit quietly and patiently while you put on their leash — then ask them to sit and calmly wait while you put on your shoes or jacket.

After you approach the door, ask them to sit again while you open the door — again after you are on the other side of the door — ask them to sit while you lock the door.

When you are methodical and deliberate and take your time with this, your dog will be able to connect the dots and will soon learn the new routine of being patient and paying attention to you.

If there are stairs or landings involved, ask them to sit at the top and also again at the bottom.

Every time you arrive at street intersection or a crosswalk, ask your Australian Labradoodle puppy to sit again, and do this in reverse when coming back home.

Also, every time you stop during your walk to speak to a neighbor, greet a friend or admire the view, ask your puppy to sit.

Every time you ask your young dog to sit for you, they are learning several things all at once — that they must remain calm while paying attention to you, that you are the boss and that they must look to you for direction and respect you as their leader. Also, a sitting puppy is much more easy to control than one standing at the alert, ready to bolt out the door or jump on someone.

Once your puppy is reliably sitting for you at least 50% of the time with voice command, also include the hand signal for "Sit", so that they will hear the word and also see the signal.

While you can use any hand signal, the universal hand signal for "Sit" is:

Right arm (palm open facing upward) parallel to the floor, and then raising your arm, while bent at the elbow toward your right shoulder.

Once your Australian Labradoodle is sitting reliable for you, remove the verbal "Sit" and replace it with the hand signal.

It's important to begin teaching hand signals during the adolescent stage of your puppy's life, because this will also help them to be more attentive and communicate in a way that is more natural for a dog — by watching you and feeling your energy, rather than always having to hear you speak a command.

As well, because the action of sitting helps to calm the mind of an excited puppy (or dog), teaching your puppy the "Sit" command is a very important part of their daily interactions with your family members as well as people you may meet when out on a walk.

When you ask your puppy to "Sit" before you interact in any way with them, before you go out or in every door, before you feed them, etc., you are helping to quiet their mind, while teaching them to look to you for direction, and at the same time making it more difficult for them to jump, lunge or disappear out a door.

The adolescent stage in a young dog's life is the perfect time to begin teaching hand signals for all your common commands, because they must look at you to understand what is expected of them, and when they are looking at you, they are more focused and less likely to take matters into their own paws.

## 10. Giving Up is Not an Option

Too often we humans get frustrated and give up on our dogs when they change from being the cute, cuddly and mostly obedient little puppy they once were, and become all kinds of trouble you never bargained for, as they grow into their adolescent stage.

Often times, it will be during the confusing adolescent stage of a dog's life that they find themselves abandoned and behind bars as their humans who promised to love and protect them, leave their once loved fur friend at the local pound or SPCA.

First of all, not all dogs go through a crazy adolescent period, and secondly, even if they do, please read this section carefully humans, because you can live through puppy adolescence and come out the other side relatively unscathed and a much more knowledgeable and patient guardian.

Congratulations are in order because you've been successful with potty training your young Australian Labradoodle puppy and with teaching them to sleep in their own kennel at night.

Further, you've lived through the teething troubles, the chewing and the hand nipping and you no longer have to get up at 3:00 a.m. to let your puppy out to go potty.

As well, you've taught your Australian Labradoodle puppy their first few basic commands, and socialized them with many other dogs, people and places, so you should feel proud of all your accomplishments and the leaps and bounds you and your puppy have accomplished together over the last several months.

Even though your adolescent puppy may be starting to act like a Tasmanian devil, and you may be having second thoughts, now is not the time to give up on them and yourself just because it may seem like someone switched your dog when you weren't looking.

Now is the time to remain calmly consistent and persistent, and to know that you will eventually be able to enjoy the happy rewards that all those months of diligent puppy training have brought to your relationship.

Yes, it can be quite a shock when what used to be your well behaved little darling who never chewed anything they weren't supposed to suddenly takes it into their head to eat all the tassels off your Persian rug or chew through a seat belt in your vehicle during the short 15 minutes you were shopping.

Even more disconcerting might be when your previously obedient and loving Australian Labradoodle puppy, who always listened to your directions, suddenly appears to have gone deaf and can't remember their name when you call them to follow you inside the house, and instead they take off running after a cat three blocks away.

And then, what happened to that quiet little puppy that never appeared to have a mean bone in their body that now spends most of their time at the window barking and growling at everything and everyone passing by?

Welcome to the world of canine adolescence where it appears that your puppy has turned into some sort of monster and all your previous hard work was for nothing. This is the time when your patience may be seriously tested.

Of coursc, this dramatic switch from bcing thc world's bcst puppy into the monster you can no longer control is not true for all puppies, as every puppy is unique.

However, being prepared for the worst will help you ride any impending storm and get you both safely out the other side where you can enjoy an even closer relationship than you previously had.

The adolescent phase may be very subtle for your Australian Labradoodle puppy or on the other hand, it may be so dramatic that you're starting to feel guilty every time you drive past the local SPCA or dog pound because thoughts of rehoming are running through your head.

If you are at the stage with your puppy that you are having great difficulties and wondering if you made the right decision to share your home with a dog, rest assured that puppy adolescence is a normal phase of their development, which can be managed, and which will definitely pass.

As well, if you are finding yourself totally overwhelmed, there are many professionals who can provide valuable assistance to help you through this stage of your puppy's development.

For most puppies, adolescence will begin between the ages of five and seven months and this is also the time that you need to be making an appointment at your veterinarian's office to have your puppy spayed or neutered.

Although neutering or spaying will not prevent undesirable adolescent behavior entirely, it can certainly reduce the intensity of it, as during this period there are hormonal changes occurring that will affect your puppy's behavior.

While it's usually hormones that are the major cause of behavioral changes in your adolescent puppy, there are also physical changes occurring at the same time that you may not be aware of.

For instance, your puppy will be going through physical growth spurts which might be causing them some pain, as well as changes related to growth in their brain while your puppy's cerebral cortex becomes more involved in thinking for itself.

Usually, during this time of brain growth, a puppy will be trying to make choices for themself, and may or may not yet be capable of making the right choices. This is why their behavior can appear to be quite erratic.

During the early adolescent period of brain development in your Australian Labradoodle puppy, the signals sometimes get mixed up and rerouted, which can result in the perplexing responses you might notice, when for instance, you ask you puppy to sit and they stare dumbly at you, even though they learned this command months ago.

Don't worry because your previous training will return.

## 11. Re-visit Basic First Commands

All that's necessary for effectively teaching your puppy their basic first commands is a calm, consistent approach, combined with your endless patience.

Many puppies are ready to begin training at about 10 to 12 weeks of age, however, be careful not to overdo it when they are less than four to six months of age, as their attention span will be short.

Make your training sessions no more than 5 or 10 minutes, positive and pleasant with lots of praise and/or treats so that your puppy will be looking forward to their next session.

Also, introduce the hand signals that go along with the verbal commands so that once they learn both, you can remove the verbal commands in favor of just hand signals.

### a) Come

While the intelligent Australian Labradoodle puppy will be capable of learning commands and tricks at a young age, the first and most important command you need to teach your puppy is the recall, or *"Come"* command.

The hand signal for "Come" is your arms spread wide open. This is a command they can see from a great distance.

Begin the "Come" command inside your home. Go into a larger room, such as your living room area. Place your puppy in front of you and attach their leash or a longer line to their Martingale collar, while you back away from them a few feet.

Say the command "Come" in an excited, happy voice and hold your arms open wide. If they do not immediately come to you, gently give a tug on the leash so that they understand that they are supposed to move toward you. When they come to you praise them and give a treat they really enjoy.

Once your puppy can accomplish a "Come" command almost every time inside your home, you can then graduate them to a nearby park or quiet outside area where you will repeat the process.

You may want to purchase an extra long, lightweight line (25 or 50 feet) so that you are always attached to your Australian Labradoodle puppy and can encourage them in the right direction should they become distracted.

**b) Sit**

The "Sit" and "Stay" commands are both easy commands to teach that will help to keep your Australian Labradoodle puppy safe and out of danger in almost every circumstance.

Find a quiet time to teach these commands when your puppy is not overly tired.

Ask your puppy to "Sit" and if they do not yet understand the command, show them what you mean by gently squeezing with your thumb and middle finger, the area across the back that joins with their back legs.

Do not just push them down into a sit as this can cause damage to their back or joints. When they sit, give them a treat and praise them. When you say the word “Sit”, at the same time show them the hand signal for this command, which is bending your arm at the elbow and raising your right hand, palm open facing upward, toward your shoulder.

### c) Stay

Once your Australian Labradoodle puppy can reliably “Sit”, say the word “Stay” and hold your outstretched arm, palm open toward their head and back away a few steps.

If they try to follow, calmly say “No” and put them back into “Sit”. Give a treat and then say again, “Stay” with the hand signal and back away a few steps.

Once your puppy is sitting and staying, you can then ask them to “Come”. Don’t forget to use the open arms hand signal for “Come.” Be a little excited with the “Come” command so that your puppy will always enjoy correctly responding and immediately returning to you.

Practice these three basic commands everywhere you go, and use the “Sit” command every time you go for a walk, before you open the door, after you are on the other side of the door, before you go down the stairs, once you are at the bottom of the stairs, and every time you stop when you are on your walk, and pretty soon you will have a puppy who automatically sits whenever you stop moving. As your puppy gets older, and their attention span increases, you will be able to train for longer periods of time.

## 12. Basic Hand Signals

Hand signal training is by far the most useful and efficient training method for every dog, including the Australian Labradoodle.

This is because all too often we inundate our canine companions with a great deal of chatter and noise that they really do not understand because English is not their first language.

Contrary to what some humans might think, the first language of an Australian Labradoodle, or any dog, is a combination of sensing energy and watching body language, which requires no spoken word or sound.

Therefore, when we humans take the time to teach our dog hand signals for all their basic commands, we are communicating with them at a level they instinctively understand, plus we are helping them to become a focused follower, as they must watch us to understand what is required of them.

**a) Come**

Come: you can kneel down for this command or stay standing. Open your arms wide like you are hugging a very large tree. This hand signal can be seen from a long distance.

When first teaching hand signals to your Australian Labradoodle, always show the hand signal for the command at the same time you say the word.

If they are totally ignoring the command, it will be time to incorporate a light lunge line, which is a very long leash to help you teach the "Come" command.

Simply attach a 20-foot line to their collar and let them sniff about in a large yard or at your neighborhood park.

At your leisure, firmly ask them to "Come" and show the hand signal. If they do not immediately come to you, give a firm tug with the lunge line, so that they understand what you are asking of them.

If they still do not "Come" toward you, simply reel them in until they are in front of you. Then let them wander about again, until you are again ready to ask them to "Come".

Repeat this process until your Australian Labradoodle responds correctly at least 80% of the time. You can also reinforce the command by giving a treat when they come back to you when asked. It is important to make sure that returning to you is always a fun, pleasant and rewarding experience for your dog or puppy. Always ask them to "Sit" when they return to you and then praise them enthusiastically.

NOTE: the "Come" command is *THE* most important command you will ever teach your dog, therefore, never ask them to come to you if you are angry or upset or to punish them in any way, because you want them to be solid with this command, and never fear coming when called.

**b) Sit**

Sit: right arm (palm open facing upward) parallel to the floor, and then raise your arm, while bent at the elbow toward your shoulder.

Sit is a very simple, yet extremely valuable command for all puppies and dogs.

If your dog is not sitting on command, try holding a treat above and slightly behind their head, so that when they look up for it they may automatically sit in order to see the treat they want.

Slowly remove the treat as reward and replace the treat with a "life reward", such as a chest rub or a scratch behind the ears and your happy smile.

If your Australian Labradoodle is not particularly treat motivated, lift up and slightly back on the leash when asking them to sit (stand in front of them), and if they still are having difficulties, reach down with your free hand, place it across your dog's back at the place where the back legs join the hip and gently squeeze.

Remember -- Do NOT simply push down on your dog's back to force their hind legs to collapse under them as this pressure could harm their spine or leg joints.

**c) Stay**

Stay: right armed fully extended toward your dog's head, palm open, hand bent up at the wrist.

Once your Australian Labradoodle is in the "Sit" position, ask them to "Stay" with both the verbal cue and the hand signal.

TIP: if you are right-handed, use your right arm and hand for the signal, and if you are left-handed, use your left arm and hand for the signal. Using your dominant hand will be much more effective because your strongest energy emanates from the palm of your dominant hand.

While your dog is sitting and staying, slowly back away from them. If they move from their position, calmly put them back into Sit and ask them to "Stay" again, using both the verbal cue and the hand signal.

Continue to practice this until your dog understands that you want them to stay sitting and not move toward you.

With all commands, when your Australian Labradoodle is just learning, be patient and always reward them with a treat and your happy praise for a job well done.

## 13. Simple Tricks

When teaching your Australian Labradoodle tricks, in order to give them extra incentive, find a treat that they really like, and give the treat as a reward and to help solidify a good performance.

Most dogs will be extra attentive during training sessions when they know that they will be rewarded with their favorite treats.

If your Australian Labradoodle is less than six months old when you begin teaching them tricks, keep your training sessions short (no more than 5 or 10 minutes) and fun, and as they become adults, you can extend your sessions as they will be able to maintain their focus for longer periods of time.

**a) Shake a Paw**

Who doesn't love a dog that knows how to shake a paw? This is one of the easiest tricks to teach your Australian Labradoodle.

TIP: most dogs are naturally either right or left pawed. If you know which paw your dog favors, ask them to shake this paw.

Find a quiet place to practice, without noisy distractions or other pets, and stand or sit in front of your dog. Place them in the sitting position and have a treat in your left hand.

Say the command *"Shake"* while putting your right hand behind their left or right paw and pulling the paw gently toward yourself until you are holding their paw in your hand. Immediately praise them and give them the treat.

Most dogs will learn the "Shake" trick quite quickly, and very soon, once you put out your hand, your Australian Labradoodle will immediately lift their paw and put it into your hand, without your assistance or any verbal cue.
Practice every day until they are 100% reliable with this trick, and then it will be time to add another trick to their repertoire.

**b) Roll Over**

You will find that just like your Australian Labradoodle is naturally either right or left pawed, that they will also naturally want to roll either to the right or the left side. Take advantage of this by asking your dog to roll to the side they naturally prefer.

Sit with your dog on the floor and put them in a lie down position. Hold a treat in your hand and place it close to their nose without allowing them to grab it, and while they are in the lying position, move the treat to the right or left side of their head so that they have to roll over to get to it.

You will very quickly see which side they want to naturally roll to, and once you see this, move the treat to this side. When they roll over to this side, immediately give them the treat and praise them.

You can say the verbal cue *"Over"* while you demonstrate the hand signal motion (moving your right hand in a circular motion) or moving the treat from one side of their head to the other with a half circle motion.

Roll Over: moving your right or left arm/hand in a small half circular motion, in the direction you wish your dog to roll toward.

Once your Australian Labradoodle can roll over every time you ask, it will be time to teach them another trick.

**c) Sit Pretty**

While this trick is a little more complicated, and most dogs pick up on it very quickly, remember that every dog is different so always exercise patience.

Find a quiet space with few distractions and sit or stand in front of your dog and ask them to "Sit".

Have a treat nearby (on a countertop or table) and when they sit, use both of your hands to lift up their front paws into the sitting pretty position, while saying the command *"Sit Pretty"*. Help them balance in this position while you praise them and give them the treat.

Once your Australian Labradoodle can do the balancing part of the trick quite easily without your help, sit or stand in front of your dog while asking them to *"Sit Pretty"* and hold the treat above their head, at the level their nose would be when they sit pretty.

TIP: when first beginning this trick, place your Australian Labradoodle beside a wall so they can use the wall to help them balance.

If they attempt to stand on their back legs to get the treat, you may be holding the treat too high, which will encourage them to stand on their back legs to reach it. Go back to the first step and put them back into the *"Sit"* position and again lift their paws while their backside remains on the floor.

Sit Pretty: hold your straight arm, fully extended, over your dog's head with a closed fist.

Make this a fun and entertaining time for your Australian Labradoodle and practice a few times every day until they can *"Sit Pretty"* on hand signal command every time you ask.

A young Australian Labradoodle puppy should be able to easily learn these basic tricks before they are six months old and when you are patient and make your training sessions short and fun for your dog, they will be eager to learn more.

## 14. Adult Training

The Australian Labradoodle is a highly intelligent, athletic breed that will be skillful in many different dog sports, therefore, in order to ensure a happy and healthy companion, make sure that you get them involved in as much activity as possible, including advanced training or canine sports.

When your Australian Labradoodle is a full grown adult (approximately two years of age), you will definitely want to begin more complicated or advanced training sessions.

They will enjoy it and when you have the desire and patience, there is no end to the commands, tricks, routines or canine sports you can teach a willing Australian Labradoodle.

For instance, you may wish to teach your adult Australian Labradoodle more advanced tricks, such as how to dance, or the opposite sided paw shakes or roll overs, which are more difficult than you might expect.

If you and your Australian Labradoodle are really enjoying learning new tricks together, you might want to advance to teaching them the hand signals for *"commando crawl"*, how to *"speak"* or to *"jump through the human hoop"*, or perhaps get them involved in a fun sport.

All of these tricks and many more are fun to teach and will exercise both your Australian Labradoodle's mind and body by taking advantage of their natural ability to excel as an entertaining circus performer.

As well, the more control you have over your Australian Labradoodle, the easier it will be to teach them a fun sport, such as Agility or Freestyle dance.

The only restriction to how far you can go with training your adult Australian Labradoodle will be your imagination and their personal ability or desire to perform, which with the exuberant Australian Labradoodle will be endless.

## 15. Behavioral Issues

It can be difficult, if not impossible to generalize or speculate with respect to alleviating possible behavioral issues or problems you may encounter with your dog because, in most cases, a dog suffering from behavioral issues requires the assistance of a dog whisperer or dog psychologist.

When reading anything about how to prevent or cure behavioral issues, please be aware that behavioral problems most often cannot be properly assessed or cured by reading a book.

The reason for this is because there are just too many variables and unique situations, individual dogs, individual humans, unique circumstances, and endless reasons why they may have developed any particular behavioral issue.

Therefore, without knowing the dog's particulars and all the history of what has transpired between the Australian Labradoodle and their guardian that came before or how the problem might have manifested itself, attempting to write about how to cure a particular issue will be no more than a best guess.

This is why someone whose dog is suffering from a specific behavioral issue that is in turn, at the least embarrassing, or at the worst dangerous, and driving the humans and the entire neighborhood crazy, must be properly addressed by engaging the services of a competent, professional dog whisperer (psychologist or behaviorist) who can ask many questions, properly assess the situation and then design a unique plan for alleviating the problem.

## 16. Overheating

### a) Outside

Be very careful, when training or walking your dog outside during hot weather, so that you do not allow them to become overheated. When it's warm outside, always carry water with you to help keep them hydrated.

TIP: if your dog has a coat that is darker colored, you can easily help to keep them cooler on hot, sunny days by having them wear a light weight vest that is a lighter color than their own coat.

Remember that smaller dogs are close to heated pavement, road surfaces or sandy beaches, which means that on a hot, sunny day, they will literally be heated from both the bottom and the top.

If the surface is very hot, do not allow them to walk on it. Instead, take them to a grassy area for their exercise.

### b) Inside Vehicles

Never leave your dog alone inside a vehicle on a warm day, even for a few minutes.

On a warm, summer day that may seem a pleasant 72°F to us humans (22.2 Celsius), inside a metal vehicle, the temperature can quickly climb to 120°F (48.8 Celsius), even with the windows left open, in a short ten minutes.

In many parts of the world it is a crime to leave a dog unattended inside a vehicle and you may return to find that your window has been broken and your dog rescued by local authorities that may have intervened, or much more serious and tragic, you may return to find that your dog has died from heat exhaustion.

As well, you might think that leaving the windows cracked and parking underneath a tree that is providing shade will be good enough for your dog. Think again, because dogs are not as efficient as humans when it comes down to regulating their body temperature and they could seriously suffer while you're off shopping or enjoying your iced latte.

A good and smart rule of thumb that will keep you and your dog safe on warm days: <u>never</u> leave them alone in your vehicle.

NOTE: also never leave your dog alone in a vehicle during cold weather because they can just as quickly suffer from hypothermia because your vehicle will turn into a large refrigerator during cold winter days just as quickly as it can turn into a deadly oven during the summer heat.

# Chapter 16: Poisonous Foods & Plants

## 1. Poisonous Foods

While some dogs are smart enough not to want to eat foods that can harm or kill them, there are those canine companions that will eat absolutely anything they can get their teeth on, whether or not it's food.

As conscientious guardians for our fur friends, it will always be our responsibility to make certain that when we share our homes with a dog, we never leave foods (or other products) that could be toxic or lethal to them easily within their reach.

While there are many foods that can be toxic to a dog, the following alphabetical list contains some of the more common foods that can seriously harm or even kill our dogs including:

Bread Dough: if your dog eats bread dough, their body heat will cause the dough to rise inside the stomach. As the dough expands during the rising process, alcohol is produced.

Dogs who have eaten bread dough may experience stomach bloating, abdominal pain, vomiting, disorientation and depression. Because bread dough can rise to many times its original size, eating only a small amount will cause a problem for any dog.

Broccoli: the toxic ingredient in broccoli is isothiocynate. While it may cause stomach upset, it probably won't be very harmful unless the amount eaten is more than 10% of the dog's total daily diet.

Chocolate: contains theobromine, a chemical that is toxic to dogs in large enough quantities. Chocolate also contains caffeine, which is found in coffee, tea, and certain soft drinks. Different types of chocolate contain different amounts of theobromine and caffeine.

For example, dark chocolate and baking chocolate or cocoa powder contain more of these compounds than milk chocolate does, therefore, a dog would need to eat more milk chocolate in order to become ill.

However, even a few ounces of chocolate can be enough to cause illness or death in a puppy or smaller dog, therefore, no amount or type of chocolate should be considered safe for a dog to eat.

A dog suffering from having eaten chocolate may display symptoms that include diarrhea, vomiting, increased heart rate, restless behavior, muscle tremors, or seizures. If they have eaten enough of it, they could die within 24 hours of eating.

During many holidays such as Christmas, New Year's, Valentine's, Easter and Halloween, chocolate is often more easily accessible to curious dogs, especially from children who are not so careful with where they might keep their Halloween or Easter egg stash and who are an easy mark for a hungry dog.

In some cases, people unwittingly poison their dogs by offering them chocolate as a treat or leaving chocolate cookies or frosted cake easily within licking distance.

Caffeine: beverages containing caffeine, such as soda, tea, coffee, and chocolate, act as a stimulant and can accelerate your dog's heartbeat to a dangerous level. Dogs eating caffeine have been known to have seizures, some of which are fatal.

Cooked Bones: can be extremely hazardous for a dog because the bones become brittle when cooked which causes them to splinter when the dog chews on them.

The splinters have sharp edges that have been known to become stuck in the teeth, and cause choking when caught in the throat or create a rupture or puncture of the stomach lining or intestinal tract.

Especially dangerous are cooked turkey and chicken legs, ham, pork chop and veal bones. Symptoms of choking include:

- Pale or blue gums
- Gasping breathing or panting
- Pawing or scratching at the face
- Slowed, shallow breathing
- Collapse and unconsciousness with dilated pupils

Grapes and Raisins: can cause acute (sudden) kidney failure in dogs. While it is not known what the toxic agent is in this fruit, clinical signs can occur within 24 hours of eating and include vomiting, diarrhea, and lethargy (tiredness).

Other signs of illness caused from eating grapes or raisins relate to the eventual shutdown of kidney functioning.

Garlic and Onions: contain chemicals that damage red blood cells by rupturing them so that they lose their ability to carry oxygen effectively, which leave the dog short of oxygen, causing what is called *"hemolytic anemia"*.

Poisoning can occur when a dog eats a large amount of garlic or onions all at once, or when eating repeated meals containing smaller amounts.

Cooking does not reduce the potential toxicity of onions and garlic.

**NOTE**: fresh, cooked, and/or powdered garlic or onions are commonly found in baby food, which is sometimes given to dogs when they are sick, therefore, be certain to carefully read food labels before feeding to your Australian Labradoodle.

Macadamia Nuts: are commonly found in candies and chocolates. Although the mechanism of macadamia nut toxicity is not well understood, the clinical signs in dogs having eaten these nuts include depression, weakness, vomiting, tremors, joint pain, and pale gums.

Signs can occur within 12 hours after eating. In some cases, symptoms can resolve themselves without treatment within 24 to 48 hours. However, keeping a close eye on your Australian Labradoodle will be strongly recommended.

Mushrooms: mushroom poisoning can be fatal if certain species of mushrooms are eaten.

The most commonly reported severely toxic species of mushroom in the US is Amanita phalloides (Death Cap mushroom), which is also quite a common species found in most parts of Britain. Other Amanita species are also toxic.

This deadly mushroom is often found growing in grassy or wooded areas near various deciduous and coniferous trees, which mean that if you're out walking with your dog in the woods, they could easily find these mushrooms.

Eating them can cause severe liver disease and neurological disorders. If you suspect your dog has eaten these mushrooms, immediately take them to your veterinarian, as the recommended treatment is to induce vomiting and to give activated charcoal. Further treatment for liver disease may also be necessary.

Pits and Seeds: many seeds and pits found in a variety of fruits, including apples, apricots, cherries, pears and plums, contain cyanogenic glycosides that can cause cyanide poisoning in your dog.

The symptoms of cyanide poisoning usually occur within 15-20 minutes to a few hours after eating and symptoms can include initial excitement, followed by rapid respiration rate, salivation or drooling, voiding of urine and feces, vomiting, muscle spasm, staggering, and coma before death.

Dogs suffering from cyanide poisoning that live more than 2 hours after onset of symptoms will usually recover.

Raw Salmon or Trout: Salmon Poisoning Disease (SPD) can be a problem for anyone who goes fishing with their dog, or feeds their dog a raw meat diet that includes raw salmon or trout.

When a snail is infected and then is eaten by the fish as part of the food chain, the dog is exposed when it eats the infected fish.

A sudden onset of symptoms can occur 5-7 days after eating the infected fish. In the acute stages, gastrointestinal symptoms are quite similar to canine parvovirus.

SPD has a mortality rate of up to 90%, can be diagnosed with a fecal sample and is treatable if caught in time.

Prevention is simple, cook all fish before feeding it to your Australian Labradoodle and immediately see your veterinarian if you suspect that your dog has eaten raw salmon or trout.

Tobacco: all forms of tobacco, including patches, nicotine gum and chewing tobacco can be fatal to dogs if eaten.

Signs of poisoning can appear quite rapidly (within an hour or less) and may include diarrhea, vomiting, a heightened state of activity, excessive drooling and panting.

Depending upon how much a dog may have eaten, more acute signs of poisoning may cause twitching, leading to collapse and coma due to heart attack that will cause death.

Never leave tobacco products within reach of your puppy or dog, and be careful not to let them pick up discarded cigarette butts when they are young puppies.

If you suspect your dog has eaten cigarette butts, seek immediate veterinary help.

**TIP**: when your dog is a very young puppy, use a double leash, collar and harness arrangement, so that you can still teach them to walk on leash with a Martingale collar around their neck, but can also attach the second leash to their harness so that you can easily lift them over enticing cigarette butts or other toxic garbage they may be trying to eat during your walks.

Tomatoes: tomatoes contain a substance called atropine, which can cause tremors, dilated pupils and an irregular heartbeat in a puppy or dog that eats them. The greatest amount of atropine will be found in the stalks and leaves of the tomato plant, next is the green tomato (before it ripens), and then ripe tomatoes.

Xylitol: is an artificial sweetener often found in many candies, gums, breath mints, toothpastes and mouthwashes that is recognized by the National Animal Poison Control Center to be a poison risk to dogs.

When puppies or dogs eat products containing Xylitol, it causes a sudden release of insulin, which in turn causes low blood sugar, which can also cause liver damage.

Within 30 minutes after eating a product containing Xylitol, the dog may vomit, be lethargic (tired), and/or be uncoordinated. However, some signs of toxicity can also be delayed for hours or even for a few days. Xylitol toxicity in dogs can be fatal if left untreated.

Please be aware that the above list is just some of the more common foods that can be toxic or fatal to our fur friends and that there are many other foods we should never be feeding our dogs.

If you have one of those dogs who will happily eat anything that looks or smells even slightly like food, or even if not food, but is enticing for a puppy or dog to eat, be certain to keep these foods or products far away from your beloved Australian Labradoodle and you'll help them to live a long and healthy life.

## 2. Poisonous Household Plants

Many common house plants are actually poisonous to our canine companions, and although many dogs simply will ignore house plants, some will attempt to eat anything, especially puppies who want to taste everything in their new world.

More than 700 plant species contain toxins that may harm or be fatal to puppies or dogs, depending on the size of the puppy or dog and how much they may eat.

Therefore, it is especially important to be aware of household plants that could be toxic when you are sharing your home with a new puppy.

Following is a short list of the more common household plants, what they look like, the different names they are known by, and what symptoms might be apparent if your puppy or dog decides to eat them.

Aloe Plant: also known as *"medicine plant or Barbados aloe"*, is a very common succulent plant that is toxic to dogs. The toxic agent in this plant is Aloin.

This bitter yellow substance is found in most aloe species and may cause vomiting and/or reddish urine.

Asparagus Fern: is also known as *"lace fern, emerald fern, emerald feather, sprengeri fern and plumosa fern"*. The toxic agent in this plant is sapogenin, which is a steroid found in a variety of plants. Repeated exposure to the berries of this plant cause vomiting, diarrhea and/or abdominal pain or skin inflammation.

Corn Plant: also known as *"ribbon plant, cornstalk plant, dragon tree and dracaena"*, is toxic to dogs. Saponin is the offensive chemical compound found in this plant. If the plant is eaten, vomiting (with or without blood), loss of appetite, depression and/or increased drooling can occur.

Cyclamen: also known as *"Sowbread",* is a pretty, flowering plant that, if eaten, can cause diarrhea, vomiting and increased salivation. If a dog eats a large amount of the plant's tubers, usually found underneath the soil at the root level, heart rhythm problems can occur, which may result in seizures or even death.

Dieffenbachia: also known as *"exotica, dumb cane and tropic snow"* contains a chemical that is a poisonous deterrent to animals. If a dog eats the plant, they will experience mouth irritation, especially on the tongue and lips that can lead to increased drooling, problems swallowing and vomiting.

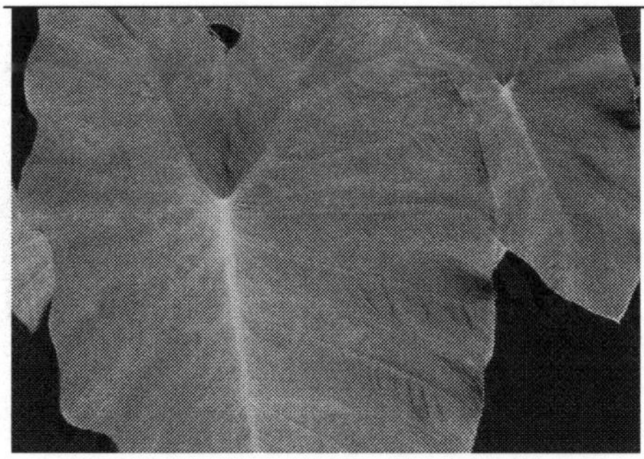

Elephant Ear: also known as *"cape, caladium, malanga, pai, taro and via sori,"* contains a chemical which is similar to a chemical also found in dieffenbachia. A dog's toxic reaction to elephant ear is similar, including oral irritation, problems swallowing, increased drooling, and vomiting.

Heartleaf Philodendron: also known as "cordatum, split-leaf philodendron, fiddle leaf, fruit salad plant, horsehead philodendron, panda plant, red emerald, red princess, and saddle leaf", is a very common, easy-to-grow houseplant that contains a chemical irritating to the mouth, tongue and lips of dogs. An affected dog may also experience difficulty swallowing, vomiting and increased drooling.

Jade Plant: has many other names, including "baby jade, Chinese rubber plant, dwarf rubber plant, friendship tree, jade tree, or Japanese rubber plant". While exactly what is toxic to dogs in this plant is unknown, a dog eating a Jade plant can suffer from loss of coordination and depression as well as a slowed heart rate.

Lilies: some plants of the lily family can be toxic to dogs. The peace lily (also known as Mauna Loa) is known to be toxic to dogs. Eating the peace lily or calla lily can cause vomiting, irritation to the dog's tongue and lips, problems swallowing and increased drooling.

Satin Pothos: (silk pothos), if eaten by a dog, the plant may cause irritation to the dog's mouth, lips and tongue, while the dog may also experience vomiting, difficulty swallowing and drooling.

The plants noted above are only a few of the more common household plants, and every conscientious Dog guardian will want to educate themselves before bringing plants into the home that could be toxic to their canine companions.

## 3. Poison Proof Your Home

You can learn about many potentially toxic and poisonous sources both inside and outside your home by visiting the ASPCA Animal Poison Control Center website.

Always keep your veterinarian's emergency number in a place where you can quickly access it, as well as the Emergency Poison Control telephone number, in case you suspect that your dog may have been poisoned.

Knowing what to do if you suspect your dog may have been poisoned and being able to quickly contact the right people could save your dog's life.

If you keep toxic cleaning substances (including fertilizers, vermin or snail poisons and vehicle products) in your home, garage or garden shed, always keep them behind closed doors.

As well, keep any medications where your Australian Labradoodle can never get to them, and seriously consider eliminating the use of any and all toxic products, for the health of both yourself, your family and your best fur friends.

## 4. Garden Plants

Please note that there are also many outdoor plants that can be toxic or poisonous to your puppy or dog, therefore, always check what plants are growing in your garden and if any may be harmful, remove them or make certain that your Australian Labradoodle puppy or adult dog cannot eat them.

Cornell University, Department of Animal Science lists many different categories of poisonous plants affecting dogs, including house plants, flower garden plants, vegetable garden plants, plants found in swamps or moist areas, plants found in fields, trees and shrubs, plants found in wooded areas, and ornamental plants.

## 5. Why Does My Dog Eat Grass?

Also, be aware that many puppies and adult dogs will eat grass, just because. Perhaps they are curious, bored, or need a little fiber in their diet.

Remember that canines are natural scavengers always on the look out for something they can eat, and so long as the grass is healthy and has not been sprayed with toxic chemicals, a little grass eating should not be a concern.

## 6. Animal Poison Control Centre

The ASPCA Animal Poison Control Center is staffed 24 hours a day, 365 days a year and is a valuable resource for learning about what plants are toxic and possibly poisonous to your dog.

**a) USA Poison Emergency**

Call: 1 (888) 426-4435

When calling the Poison Emergency number, your credit card may be charged with a $65. ((£39.42) consultation fee.

**b) UK Poison Emergency**

Call: 0800-213-6680 - Pet Poison Helpline (payable service)

Call: 0300 1234 999 - RSPCA

ASPCA Poison Control: **www.aspca.org**

# Chapter 17: Caring for Aging Dogs

## 1. What to Be Aware Of

As a result of many modern advances in veterinarian care, improvements in diet and nutrition and general knowledge concerning proper care of our canine companions, our dogs are able to enjoy longer, healthier lives.

As such, when caring for our canine companions, we need to be aware of behavioral and physical changes that will affect our dogs as they approach old age.

While each dog's individual health, genetics, and spirit will affect how old they seem, and they may remain quite as they get older active, a Australian Labradoodle will be entering their senior years at around 8 to 10 years of age.

### a) Physiological Changes

As our beloved canine companions enter into their senior years, they may be suffering from very similar, physical aging problems that affect us humans, such as pain, stiffness and arthritis, and inability to control their bowels and bladder.

Any of these problems will reduce a dog’s willingness to want to exercise.

### b) Behavioral Changes

Further, a senior Australian Labradoodle may experience behavioral changes resulting from loss of hearing and sight, such as disorientation, fear or startle reactions and overall grumpiness from any number of physical problems that could be causing them pain whenever they move.

Just as research and science has improved our human quality of life in our senior years, the same is becoming true for our canine counterparts who are able to benefit from dietary supplements and pharmaceutical products to help them be as comfortable as possible in their senior years.

Of course, there will be some inconveniences associated with keeping a dog with advancing years around the home, however, your Australian Labradoodle deserves no less than to spend their final days in your loving care after they have unconditionally given you their entire lives.

**c) Geriatric Dogs**

Being aware of the changes that are likely occurring in a senior dog will help you to better care for them during their geriatric years.

For instance, most dogs will experience hearing loss and visual impairment, and how you help them will depend upon which goes first (hearing or sight).

For instance, if a dog's hearing is compromised, then using more hand signals will be helpful.

Deaf dogs will still be able to hear louder noises and feel vibrations, therefore hand clapping, knocking on walls, doors or furniture, using a loud clicker or stomping your foot on the floor may be a way to get their attention.

If a senior dog loses their eyesight, most dogs will still be able to easily navigate their familiar surroundings, and you will only need to be extra watchful on their behalf when taking them to unfamiliar territory.

If they still have their hearing, you will be able to assist your dog with verbal cues and commands.

Dogs that have lost both their hearing and their sight will need to be close to you so that they can relax and not feel nervous, and so that you can communicate by touching parts of their body.

Generally speaking, even when a dog becomes blind and/or deaf, their powerful sense of smell is still functioning, which means that they will be able to smell where you are and navigate their environment by using their nose.

**d) More Bathroom Breaks**

Bathroom breaks may need to become more frequent in older dogs who may lose their ability to hold it for longer periods of time, so be prepared to be more watchful and to offer them opportunities to go outside more frequently during the day.

You may also want to place a pee pad near the door, in case they just can't hold it long enough, or if you have not already taught them to bathroom on an indoor potty patch, or pee pad, now may be the time for this alternative bathroom arrangement.

A dog who has been house trained for years will feel the shame and upset of not being able to hold it long enough to get to their regular bathroom location, so be kind and do whatever you need to do in order to help them not to have to feel bad about failing bowel or bladder control.

Our beloved canine companions may also begin to show signs of cognitive decline and changes in the way their brain functions, similar to what happens to humans suffering from Alzheimer's, where they start to wander about aimlessly, sometimes during the middle of the night. Make sure that if this is happening with your senior Australian Labradoodle at nighttime, that they cannot accidentally fall down stairs or harm themselves in any way.

Being aware that an aging Australian Labradoodle will be experiencing many symptoms that are similar to an aging human will help you to understand how best to keep them safe and as comfortable as possible during this golden time in their lives.

## 2. How to Make Them Comfortable

### a) Regular Checkups

During this time in your Australian Labradoodle's life, when their immune systems become weakened and they may be experiencing pain, you will want to get into the habit of taking your senior Australian Labradoodle for regular veterinarian checkups. Take them for a checkup every six months so that early detection of any problems can quickly be attended to and solutions for helping to keep your aging Australian Labradoodle comfortable can be provided.

### b) No Rough Play

An older Australian Labradoodle will not have the same energy or willingness to play that they did when they were younger, therefore, do not allow younger children to rough house with an older dog. Explain to them that the dog is getting older and that as a result they must learn to be gentle and to leave the dog alone when it may want to rest or sleep.

### c) Mild Exercise

Dogs still love going for walks, even when they are getting older and slowing down. Although an older Australian Labradoodle will generally have less energy, they still need to exercise and keep moving, and taking them out regularly for shorter or slower walks will keep them healthier and happier long into old age.

### d) Best Quality Food

Everyone has heard the saying, *"you are what you eat"* and for a senior dog, what he or she eats is even more important as his or her digestive system may no longer be functioning at peak performance.

Therefore, feeding a high quality, protein-based food will be important for a senior dog's continued health.

As well, if your older Australian Labradoodle is overweight, you will want to help them shed excess pounds so that they will not be placing undue stress on their joints or heart.

The best way to accomplish this is by feeding smaller quantities of a higher quality food.

**e) Clean and Parasite Free**

The last thing an aging Australian Labradoodle should have to deal with is the misery of itching and scratching, so make sure that you continue to give them regular baths with the appropriate shampoos and conditioners to keep their coat and skin comfortable and free from biting bugs.

**f) Plenty of Water**

Proper hydration is essential for helping to keep an older Australian Labradoodle comfortable.

Water is life giving for every creature, so make certain that your aging dog has easy access to plenty of clean, fresh water which will help to improve their energy and digestion and also prevent dehydration which can add to joint stiffness.

**g) Keep Them Warm**

Just as older humans feel the cold more, so do older dogs. Keeping your senior Australian Labradoodle warm will help to alleviate some of the pain of their joint stiffness or arthritis. Make sure their bed or kennel is not kept in a drafty location and perhaps consider a heated bed for them.

Be aware that your aging Australian Labradoodle will be more sensitive to extremes in temperature, and it will be up to you to make sure that they are comfortable at all times, which means not too hot and not too cold.

**h) Indoor Clothing**

We humans tend to wear warmer clothing as we get older, simply because we have more difficulty maintaining a comfortable body temperature and the same will be true of our senior Australian Labradoodle companions.

Therefore, while you most likely already have a selection of outdoor clothing appropriate to the climate in which you live, you may not have considered keeping your Australian Labradoodle warm while inside the home.

Now would be the time to consider doggy t-shirts or sweater clothing options to help keep your aging companion comfortably warm both inside and out.

**i) Steps or Stairs**

If your Australian Labradoodle is allowed to sleep on the human couch or chair, but they are having difficulties getting up there as their joints are becoming stiff and painful, consider buying or making them a set of soft, foam stairs so that they do not have to make the jump to their favorite sleeping place.

**j) Comfortable Bed**

While most dogs seem to be happy with sleeping on the floor, providing a padded, soft bed will greatly help to relieve sore spots and joint pain in older dogs.

If there is a draft in the home, generally it will be at floor level, therefore, a bed that is raised up off of the floor will be warmer for your senior Australian Labradoodle.

### k) More Love and Attention

Last, but not least, make sure that you give your senior Australian Labradoodle lots of love and attention and never leave them alone for long periods of time.

When they are not feeling their best, they will want to be with you all that much more because you are their trusted guardian whom they love beyond life itself.

## 3. What is Euthanasia?

Every veterinarian will have received special training to help provide all incurably ill, injured or aged pets that have come to the end of their natural lives with a humane and gentle death, through a process called *"euthanasia"*.

When the time comes, euthanasia, or putting a dog *"to sleep"*, will usually be a two-step process.

First, the veterinarian will inject the dog with a sedative to make them sleepy, calm and comfortable.

Second, the veterinarian will inject a special drug that will peacefully stop their heart.

These drugs work in such a way that the dog will not experience any awareness whatsoever that their life is transitioning toward a peaceful ending. What they will experience is very much like what we humans experience when falling asleep under anesthesia during a surgical procedure.

Once the second stage drug has been injected, the entire process takes about 10 to 20 seconds, at which time the veterinarian will then check to make certain that the dog's heart has stopped.

There is no suffering with this process, which is a very gentle and humane way to end a dog's suffering and allow them to peacefully pass on.

## 4. When to Help a Dog Transition

The impending loss of a beloved dog is one of the most painfully difficult and emotionally devastating experiences a canine guardian will ever have to face.

For the sake of our faithful companions, because we do not want to prolong their suffering, we humans will have to do our best to look at our dog's situation practically, rather than emotionally, so that we can make the best decision for them.

They may be suffering from extreme old age and the inability to even walk outside to relieve themselves, and thus having to deal with the indignity of regularly soiling their sleeping area, they may have been diagnosed with an incurable illness that is causing them much pain, or they may have been seriously injured.

Whatever the reason for a canine companion's suffering, it will be up to their human guardian to calmly guide the end-of-life experience so that any further discomfort and distress can be minimized.

### a) What to Do If You Are Uncertain

In circumstances where it is not entirely clear how much a dog is suffering, it will be helpful to pay close attention to your Australian Labradoodle's behavior and keep a daily log or record so that you can know for certain how much of their day is difficult and painful for them, and how much is not.

When you keep a daily log, it will be easier to decide if the dog's quality of life has become so poor that it makes better sense to offer them the gift of peacefully going to sleep.

During this time of uncertainty, it will also be very important to discuss with your veterinarian what signs of suffering may be associated with the dog's particular disease or condition, so that you know what to look for.

Often a dog may still continue to eat or drink despite being upset, having difficulty breathing, excessively panting, being disoriented or in much pain, and as their caring guardians, we will have to weigh their love of eating against how much they are really suffering in all other aspects of their life.

Obviously, if a canine guardian can clearly see that their beloved companion is suffering throughout their days and nights, it will make sense to help humanely end their suffering by planning a euthanasia procedure.

We humans are often tempted to delay the inevitable moment of euthanasia, because we love our dogs so much and cannot bear the anticipation of the intense grief we know will overwhelm us when we must say our final goodbyes to our beloved fur friend.

Unfortunately, we may regret that we allowed our dog to suffer too long, and could find ourselves wishing that if only we humans had the same option, to peacefully let go, when we find ourselves in such a stage in our own lives.

## 5. Grieving a Lost Pet

Some humans do not fully recognize the terrible grief involved in losing a beloved canine friend.

There will be many who do not understand the close bond we humans can have with our dogs, which is often unlike any we have with our human counterparts.

Your friends may give you pitying looks and try to cheer you up, but if they have never experienced such a loss themselves, they may also secretly think that you are making too much fuss over "just a dog".

For some of us humans, the loss of a beloved dog is so painful that we decide never to share our lives with another, because we cannot bear the thought of going through the pain of loss again.

Expect to feel terribly sad, tearful and yes, depressed because those who are close to their canine companions will feel their loss no less acutely than the loss of a human friend or life partner.

The grieving process can take some time to recover from, and some of us never totally recover.

After the loss of a family dog, first you need to take care of yourself by making certain that you keep eating and getting regular sleep, even though you will feel an almost eerie sense of loneliness.

Losing a beloved dog is a shock to the system, which can also affect your concentration and your ability to find joy or want to participate in other activities that may be part of your daily life.

During this early grieving time you will need to take extra care while driving or performing tasks that require your concentration as you may find yourself distracted.

If there are other dogs or pets in the home, they will also be grieving the loss of a companion, and may display this by acting depressed, being off their food or showing little interest in play or games. Therefore, you need to help guide your other pets through this grieving process by keeping them busy and interested, taking them for extra walks and spending more time with them.

Many people do not wait long enough before attempting to replace a lost pet and will immediately go to the local shelter and rescue a deserving dog.

While this may help to distract you from your grieving process, this is not really fair to the new fur member of your family.

Bringing a new pet into a home that is depressed and grieving the loss of a long time canine member may create behavioral problems for the new dog who will be faced with learning all about their new home while also dealing with the unstable, sad energy of the grieving family.

A better scenario would be to allow yourself the time to properly grieve by waiting a minimum of one month to allow yourself and your family to feel happier and more stable before deciding upon sharing your home with another dog.

The grieving process will be different for everyone and you will know when the time is right to consider sharing your home with another canine companion.

## 6. The Rainbow Bridge Poem

"Just this side of heaven is a
place called Rainbow Bridge.

When an animal dies that has been
especially close to someone here,
that pet goes to Rainbow Bridge.
There are meadows and hills for all of our special friends
so they can run and play together.
There is plenty of food, water and sunshine,
and our friends are warm and comfortable.

All the animals who had been ill and old
are restored to health and vigor;
those who were hurt or maimed
are made whole and strong again,
just as we remember them in our dreams
of days and times gone by.

The animals are happy and content,
except for one small thing;
they each miss someone very special to them,
who had to be left behind.

They all run and play together,
but the day comes when one suddenly stops
and looks into the distance.
His bright eyes are intent; His eager body quivers.
Suddenly he begins to run from the group,
flying over the green grass,
his legs carrying him faster and faster.

You have been spotted,
and when you and your special friend finally meet,
you cling together in joyous reunion,
never to be parted again.
The happy kisses rain upon your face;
your hands again caress the beloved head,
and you look once more into the trusting eyes
of your pet, so long gone from your life
but never absent from your heart.

Then you cross Rainbow Bridge together...."

- Author unknown

## 7. Memorials

There are as many ways to honor the passing of a beloved pet, as each of our fur friends is uniquely special to us.

For instance, you and your family may wish to have your companion cremated and preserve their ashes in a special urn or sprinkle their ashes along their favorite walk, or across the lake where they loved to swim.

Perhaps you will want to have a special marker, photo bereavement, photo engraved Rainbow Bridge Poem, or wooden plaque created in honor of your passed friend.

You may wish to keep their memory close to you at all times by having a DNA remembrance pendant or bracelet designed.

As well, there are support groups, such as Rainbow Bridge, which is a grief support community, to help you and your family through this painful period of loss and grief.

# Chapter 18: Rescue Organizations

When you are considering rescuing a specific breed of dog or puppy, the first place to start your search will be with your local breeders, shelters and rescue groups.

There are many breed specific rescue organizations in Canada, the USA, the United Kingdom and many other countries and the easiest way to find one closest to you is to go online and type in the breed name of the dog you want to rescue next to the name of the city where you live.

As well, if you have the free Dogalize app on your smart device, you will be able to easily search for rescues in your specific area and see pictures of available dogs.

## 1. Shelters

Here you can expect to pay an adoption fee to cover the cost of spaying or neutering, but this will be only a small percentage of what you would pay a breeder, and you will be saving a life at the same time.

## 2. Online Resources

Sites such as Petango, Adopt A Pet and Pet Finder can be good places to begin your search.

Each of these online resources is a central gathering site for hundreds and hundreds of local shelters, humane societies and rescue groups.

## 3. Canine Clubs and Breeders

Another place to search will be hybrid clubs or breeders in your local area. These groups may have rescue dogs available.

# Chapter 19: Resources & References

The following resources and references are listed alphabetically within their specific category and include web addresses.

ASPCA Poison Control: www.aspca.org
Poisonous Plants Affecting Dogs - Cornell University, Department of Animal Science
www.ansi.cornell.edu/plants/dogs/

## 1. Breeders, Registries & Rescues

Adopt A Pet: www.adoptapet.com
Aladdin Labradoodles: www.aladdinlabradoodles.com
Australian Labradoodles of Windsor Creek:
www.australianlabradoodlesofwindsorcreek.com
Breeders Club: www.breedersclub.net/html/breeds/Beagle.htm
CreamofBritish Australian Labradoodles: www.creamofbritish-australianlabradoodles.com
Manorborn Australian Labradoodles: www.manorborn-australian-labradoodles.com
National Dog Tattoo Register: www.dog-register.co.uk
National Dog Registry: www.nationaldogregistry.com
Petango: www.petango.com
Pet Finder: www.petfinder.com
The American Kennel Club: www.akc.org
The Australian Labradoodle Club:
www.australianlabradoodleclub.us
The Kennel Club: www.thekennelclub.org.uk
UK Australian Labradoodle Club:
http://www.ukaustralianlabradoodleclub.co.uk

## 2. Equipment, Supplies & Services

Andis Dog Clippers: www.andis.com
Dog Bowl for Your Dog: www.dogbowlforyourdog.com

Dogalize, the dog lover's free app: www.dogalize.com
Dremel™ Nail Grinder for Dogs: www.dremel.com
K-9 Super Heroes Dog Whispering:
www.k-9superheroesdogwhispering.com
Modern Puppies: www.modernpuppies.com
Oster Dog Clippers: www.osterpro.com
Potty Patch: www.pottypatch.com
Poochie Bells™: www.poochie-pets.net
Remove Urine Odors: www.removeurineodors.com
Sleepy Pod: www.sleepypod.com
Tell Bell™: www.tellbell.com
Tick Twister: www.ticktwister.com
ThunderShirt: www.thundershirt.com
Wahl Dog Clippers: www.wahl.com

## 3. Memorials

Rainbow Bridge: www.rainbowbridge.com

**Published by Zoodoo Publishing 2023**

Printed in Great Britain
by Amazon

4490682b-38dc-414d-bdaa-c6055380a643R01